MY
SIGNIFICANT
Nobody

MY
SIGNIFICANT
Nobody

STEVIE D. PARKER

atmosphere press

Dedicated to My Significant Somebody

Chapter One

AMBER

Finishing up spraying my hair, I studied myself in the mirror. It was such a pain to put curls in my hair, but somehow, still worth it in the end. I started shuffling through my jewelry box for a bracelet to accessorize my outfit. I was kind of relieved I had to work after this party; it gave me an excuse to wear black. Not many colors looked right on me as my hair was red. The fact that my eyes are a dull brown didn't help much either.

Evan gazed up at me from his video game as I walked out into the living room to find my pocketbook. He looked me up and down with a look of confusion on his face.

"You're wearing that to work?" He asked, sounding surprised.

As he checked me out, my eyes scanned the room. It was a mess, as usual. Evan was such a slob; it became hard to live with him at times. The living room was small, but I had decorated it nicely with an L-shaped couch that fit perfectly under the window, facing the TV hanging on the wall. The other corner where he insisted on displaying his drum set, which he could never use because our neighbors would complain, would be where the crib would eventually go. Not only was I a neat freak, but I was also a chronic planner.

From the moment we started dating five years ago, I knew when I would expect a ring, what month our wedding would be in, and when we would try to have our first kid. With the wedding only six months away, I was on schedule to get pregnant by next year, and that drum set would finally have to go.

I placed my pocketbook over my shoulder, let out a sigh, and looked directly into his brown eyes. For a thirty-year-old, he looked a lot older than he was. His stomach was already protruding a bit, and he wasn't very tall, making him appear stockier than he was. With his dark hair sprinkled with grays and thick-rimmed black glasses on, he looked closer to forty.

"This place is a mess, Evan! I'm going to Bianca's birthday party. I've told you that a thousand times already."

"Oh right," he began, his attention now turned to the video game. "Where is it again?"

"That new Asian fusion restaurant downtown. Isabel knew a guy there and was able to get us in. Do you like my hair?"

Pausing the game, Evan looked up at my hair. He was

scanning it thoroughly, trying to figure out what was different. "It's nice," he finally said.

I smiled. "What did I do to it?" I asked.

He put the controller down on the coffee table and ran his hand from the back of his hair to his neck. He raised his eyebrows, looking me up and down. He sat silent for a second and then said, "You dyed it."

I let out a laugh and turned around towards the door. "I'm going to work after the party. I'll be home around five or six in the morning."

I hailed a cab and instructed him to make a stop along the way to pick up Mia. She only lived four blocks from me. Mia was my best friend. We had grown up in New Jersey and had known each other since middle school. We always thought we would be journalists and move to New York City together. She moved to New York before I did. That hadn't been part of the plan but when my mother got so sick, I had to stay with her. I moved three years after Mia. I finally had to put my mother into an adult home for the mentally disabled when it became too much to take care of her myself anymore. It wasn't long after Mia and I became roommates that I had met Evan, who I eventually moved in with.

Neither of us became journalists, but Mia was able to get me a bartending job with her boss's brother, James. The Nisan brothers were well known in New York City for both their bars and playboy-type lifestyles. They had inherited the bars from their father, but both bars were entirely different scenes.

Rob's bar was more of a lounge. Bottle service and VIP tables, wealthy clientele. James' bar was more of a laid-back sports bar. TVs in every corner viewing all the different games playing that night, sports memorabilia hung along the walls, and board games at the tables for the younger crowd. As we were not far from Wall Street, we had a lot of stockbrokers come in for happy hour.

When the taxi pulled up, Mia was already standing outside clenching her peacoat together. It didn't take her long to jump in the car.

"Shit, it's fucking freezing out. I don't remember it being so cold in February. When is spring going to come already?" She exclaimed, slamming the door. As I went to open my mouth, she put her finger up to indicate to be quiet. "Hold on one sec, let me text Rob and remind him I'll be in late," she said.

She had a point. James would probably forget I was going to be in late also. I looked in my phone for his number, listed under "Biggest Asshole." I typed: *just a reminder I will be late today. Probably around eleven.* Mia looked up from her phone, finally looking at me. "You look great!"

"Thanks, so do you!" I said.

Mia was always the prettiest girl in school. She had long blonde hair, blue eyes, and a body that would make anyone think she spent all day in a gym. She was blessed with genes that allowed her to look like that without having to work for it. I always had to watch what I ate to keep slim, I was so envious of how she could eat whatever she wanted without any repercussions.

When we got to the restaurant, the rest of the party was already seated. The hostess led us through the room. The loud dance music that was blaring, made the place appear more like a club than a restaurant and the walls shimmered with red and gold Asian carvings. The bar was pretty cool as well. It changed colors every few minutes and illuminated the bottles of alcohol in whatever shade was shining through.

"Happy Birthday, Bianca!" We seemed to say in sync as we sat down. Mia picked up the ceramic chopsticks in front of her as the waitress took our drink orders.

"Does everyone know how to use these?" Mia asked, looking up embarrassed.

"Not everyone can get away with eating fast food every day," Bianca said, giggling.

"Well, we can. We just have to work out like beasts," Matt chimed in.

Bianca and Matt were Broadway actors, while both Isabel and Stacey were strippers. All of us had nighttime jobs, making it easier for us to make plans with each other than with nine to five people. The night was daytime to us and the day night. It was hard to have relationships outside this group because we ran on such different schedules, unlike the rest of the world. I had remembered the night we met them, out at a club. We had been so excited to meet other people that we would be able to go out with.

"I have to tell you guys about this guy last night!" Isabel said after our drinks had arrived and we put in our food orders. "So, I met this guy online," she continued. "Firefighter, hot as fuck. Gorgeous blue eyes and a body that could literally be made of steel."

"Was he really *hot*, or was it just the uniform?" Bianca asked.

"No, no, he was insanely hot. So anyway, as I'm in an Uber on the way to his house, because of course my luck he lives in Brooklyn, he starts sending me these texts, telling me he's been bad, needs to be punished...."

"Oh God, S&M?" Stacey speculated.

Isabel shook her head. "Nope, not even. I get to his house, and..." she paused. We all leaned in, now incredibly curious at what was going to come out of her mouth. "Ready for it?"

She lingered a little longer for dramatic effect. "Well?" Matt asked impatiently.

"I get into his house, and he's in a diaper, pacifier in his mouth! He reminded me what a bad boy he was and how he needed a lesson."

I nearly spit my drink out. "Shut up," I said. "No way! You're lying."

She shook her head and raised her hand in a swear position. "I'm not. He wanted me to change his diaper!"

"What did you do?" Stacey asked. Isabel took a sip of her drink and shrugged her shoulders.

"I changed his diaper. I had just spent twenty bucks to get there, and I wasn't leaving. But I'll tell you one thing; I'm certainly never answering his texts again."

We all started laughing as the waitress arrived and slid our entrees in front of us. My phone vibrated as *Biggest Asshole* came across my phone. I looked down to read the text.

I know you told me three times.

"Speaking of freaks, how's James?" Isabel asked, noticing he had texted me. Isabel had a thing for James ever since I met her. She was stunning, Spanish, and curvy, with blue eyes so bright they appeared to sparkle. James always seemed to show her extra attention when she came into the bar. I was so jealous of her confidence. She was hot, and she knew it. Men always stumbled over themselves for her.

"He's fine," I simply answered, picking up a piece of sushi.

"Now I heard *he's* a freak," Stacey said.

"So is his brother," Mia answered.

"No, like the real deal, hardcore freak. I heard he gets off on getting girls to do things they never thought they would do. But he doesn't ask them to do it. Like he has some sort of mind manipulation over women that make them suddenly want to do whatever he wants," Stacey said.

"I heard he's huge too," Isabel added, grinning. The truth was, most girls liked James. He was tall, built, charismatic. Gorgeous blue eyes with black hair and seemed to always to have a five o'clock shadow. He made a lot of money from the bar, and he was quite the charmer. Both his forearms were covered in tattoos, and he was incredibly in shape. He was also such a good talker, I had never witnessed a girl turn him down.

"So, would you change his diaper?" Matt asked Isabel. Bianca slapped Matt on the shoulder.

"Gross!" She said, grimacing. "Is it true he video-tapes?" She asked, now looking at me. "That's what Gina from the club told me," I swallowed my sushi.

"Okay, I just work for the guy. It's not like he comes into work and shows me videos from the night before. Can we change the subject, please? I have to see him in a few hours. I don't need to be visualizing his body parts!"

I would love to say that the conversation changed its course, but it didn't. Most of the time, they talked about rumors they heard of James, and when it finally did change, it went into other sex stories. Not one story I could tell came close to any of the stories the others had. I had been with Evan for so long, and it wasn't as if we were having much sex lately.

We had a good time, though, and the food was terrific. When Bianca had gone out with Isabel to smoke a cigarette, Isabel must have mentioned Bianca's birthday to the waitress because as they sat back down, a birthday cake arrived. We all sang happy birthday, gave Bianca her gifts, and departed to go to work. It was only ten-thirty, and my night was just beginning.

Chapter Two

I got to the bar at almost eleven. It was relatively packed for a Thursday night. I pushed past the crowd and ducked behind the bar where James had five glasses lined up in front of him as he made drinks. I caught eye contact with a girl motioning for me. She ordered two "flaming marshmallows," a drink I hated making with a passion, and had begged James to remove from the drink menu numerous times. I stood next to James as I went to make these ridiculous drinks.

"What are you doing here?" I asked, my eyes focused on the glasses in front of me. He slid the glasses across the bar, took the cash from the customer, and turned around to the register. James only worked on Friday and Saturday nights. On Thursdays and Sundays, I worked with Kaitlyn.

"I own the place," he said, counting change and not

looking up. "You told me three times you were going to be late."

He reappeared with change for the customer. Then, with my back to him, getting change for my customer, I replied, "Oh, I just assumed you'd get Bruce to come in."

As I came back to the front of the bar to hand over the change, our eyes finally met. "It was only three hours. Why pay someone for what I can do myself?" He paused, looking at me intently. "You do something different with your hair?"

I touched my hair. Until he mentioned it, I completely forgot I had curled it.

"Yeah, I dyed it," I sarcastically answered. I surveyed the customers to see if anyone needed a drink, but everyone was content at the moment.

He turned his whole body around and examined my hair.

"No, you didn't. You curled it," he said.

I tilted my head and looked up at him.

"You noticed I curled it?" I asked.

"I mean, it's an obvious difference. It's usually pin-straight. I like it."

I looked down. He exhaled and came closer to me.

"What? What did I say?" He asked.

"Nothing. You're right; I curled it. It's just, well...."

He took a step back and put his hands in his pockets.

"Evan didn't even notice," I admitted.

"Oh, well, I mean Evan sees you all the time in all different scenarios. After the shower, after he bangs you out...."

"Bangs me out?" I interrupted.

"Yeah, he bangs you out, right? Please tell me he bangs

you out because if he doesn't, I am telling you right now, your relationship is doomed."

A young guy gestured to me from across the bar. After he ordered a gin and tonic, I returned to the soda machine where James was still standing.

"You need a girlfriend, *badly*," I said.

"A girlfriend!" He exclaimed as if I insulted him. I handed the customer his drink and took his money to go to the register.

"Yes, a girlfriend. Someone to make a decent guy out of you," I said and returned to give the customer his change. James lifted his shirt to expose his six-pack.

"Touch it," he said. I wrapped my arms around my chest and looked up into his eyes. Suddenly all I could picture was the girls talking about how well-endowed he was.

"Go ahead. Touch it," he insisted, smiling. I ran my hand across his stomach. I have to admit; it was solid and unbelievably sexy.

"Ohhhh, so sexy," I exaggeratingly said.

He tucked his shirt back in.

"Amber, I'm thirty-five years old and in the prime of my life. Why would I want a girlfriend to tie me down? Speaking of girls and tying down, how's my Bella?"

I rolled my eyes. "James, look around. There are hundreds of girls in New York City that would be more than willing to sleep with you. So why do you have to go after my friends?"

"Why are you so opposed to Isabel and me hooking up?" He asked. I will admit, James and Isabel looked perfect for each other. They would make a good couple, but only visibly. They were too much alike. It would have been a disaster if they hooked up, and it was too close to home to chance it.

"You and Isabel are like thunder and lightning. It's a train wreck in the making."

"I have to be honest, you not wanting me to sleep with her makes me want to sleep with her more," he confessed. "And doesn't thunder and lightning go well together?" I just shook my head and ignored his statement.

By two a.m., the unusually busy Thursday night started slowing down. A few guys were left at the bar, along with a table of four girls who were sipping their drinks and munching on nachos. This, however, did not stop our playful banter from continuing throughout the night.

"She's definitely a take-charge type of girl. I'd probably be the one tied up," he commented.

"Are you back on Isabel?" I asked, now pouring myself a drink. He was a cool boss. He didn't care if we drank behind the bar, as long as we paced ourselves.

Kaitlyn cleared her throat to indicate she was standing there waiting to leave. James went to the register, paid her, and continued right on after she left without skipping a beat. "I'd love to be on Isabel. So, is that a yes?" He asked, now making himself a drink also.

"What makes you so sure she's 'take charge'? I bet she's quite the opposite. Prefers that you make love to her and cuddle after. You still down?" I asked, taking a sip of my drink. He started shaking his head.

"No, she's not. I know these things. It's like a superhero ability." Stopping, James looked over at the table where the four girls were, nodding his head in their direction. "See the girl over there? The blonde with the glasses. Looks real quiet and shy right? No, she's just the opposite. Once those glasses come off, she's a screamer," he said, now leaning over the bar, resting his chin in his hands.

"You slept with her, didn't you?" I asked. He straightened himself back up, looking at me.

"No, not yet." He went into his pocket, took out a wad of cash tightly secured with a rubber band, and put a twenty-dollar bill on the bar. "But twenty bucks says I can, and she is."

"Haven't you ever heard of a wallet?" I asked.

"I have a wallet," he said, reaching into his back pocket and revealing the black leather beat-up case. "My money just doesn't fit in here. The problems of having a cash business. This is just for my important stuff." He started rifling through the contents in the wallet to show me. "ID, credit card, condom," he winked. I rolled my eyes as he put the wallet back in his pocket.

I looked over at the twenty-dollar bill on the bar and then back at him. "You're on."

I watched him as he made his way around the bar and approached the girls. He took a bar stool from a table next to them and sat between them, staring intensely at the girl in the glasses. Leaned on the high-top table, his biceps hardened through his black t-shirt. He reeked of confidence, but not in an arrogant type of way. More of a sexy, charming kind of way. I watched the girl look down shyly, then take out her phone. I couldn't hear what they were saying, but she immediately put her phone back away without taking his number. A few minutes later, he returned to the bar.

"Struck out?" I asked, going to take the twenty off the

bar. He put his hand on top of it and held it on the bar before I could take it.

"Not so fast. I told her I don't do phone numbers, and I get off in half an hour."

We both took our hands off the twenty and left it there. After the last round was called, as I had my back to him counting money, I heard him say, "Should I take this now, or do you want to wait to hear the story tomorrow?"

When I turned around, he was on the other side of the bar, sitting on a stool. Sure enough, the girl in the glasses was standing by the door waiting for him.

I looked at her, then to him, now holding the money and waving it at me. He winked.

"Take it now. I'll close up," I said.

He went into his pocket and took back out his bundle of cash and put the twenty back in with it. "See you tomorrow. By the way, you should really wear dresses more often. You look good in them," he said as he made his way to meet the girl.

I got home a little after six a.m., and Evan was already getting dressed for work.

"Did you ask about next Friday?" He asked me as he was buttoning up his shirt in the mirror.

"No, I already told you I couldn't take it off," I replied, slipping off my dress and pulling up pajama pants. He stopped buttoning his shirt and turned around to face me.

"How do you know that if you didn't ask?" He said.

"Evan," I began, "I cannot afford to take time off from work. Between the gynecologist last month and the wedding, I need the money."

"You would have already been on my insurance had you just...." I cut him off before he could finish.

"I already told you I am not getting married at City Hall! The one thing I wanted my whole life was a nice wedding. Why can't you understand that?" I asked.

"And the one thing I wanted was a significant other to bring to company events. Why can't *you* understand *that*?" He threw back. "Why are you even still there? What was the sense of going to all those years of school for a journalism degree just to bartend? What happened to your 'plan'?"

I pulled a t-shirt over my head and put on my room-darkening eye mask.

"Do you know how much writers make starting out? Once the wedding is over, I will quit and look for a writing job. I'm too tired to argue about this now," I said and crawled under the covers. This had been an ongoing disagreement for a few years now; he hated that I bartended. A few minutes later, I heard the door shut behind him.

The next night, as I stood at the bar cutting limes, I couldn't get our conversation out of my head. This was the third company event Evan had to go to that I wasn't able to attend. Had any of these events been on a regular weeknight, I could have gone, but Fridays were always a big money-making night for me. I could make five hundred dollars on a Friday night. That was a lot of cash to disregard for a stupid work event that wasn't even my own. Finally, James snapped me back into reality as he threw a twenty-dollar bill on the bar.

"Here's your money, no questions," he sternly said.

I took the money and put it in my pocket, looking up at him.

"Not a screamer, I take it?"

He came around the back of the bar.

"That sounds like a question to me," he replied.

I started laughing. He was obviously annoyed, which somehow made me forget my Evan issue. "C'mon, spill it!" I egged him on.

He started taking the glasses out of the dishwasher under the bar and placed them on the shelf. Without looking up, he said, "No, she was a screamer, alright. She yelled so loudly at me, I'm surprised you didn't hear her from your apartment."

I put the knife down and turned around to face him, leaning my back against the bar.

"What did you do?" I questioned curiously.

He looked up at me and bit his bottom lip. "You were right. I did sleep with her," he said casually.

I covered my mouth in complete shock.

"Seriously? I was only kidding! When? How did you forget? What made you remember?" I rattled out questions, suddenly very fascinated.

"I don't know. A few years ago. She told me to do 'that thing' she likes. When I tried to guess what she was referring to, I was completely off, and she went nuts," he said, clenching his teeth. "In my defense, she was a redhead then, and now she's blonde."

"Well, now I kinda want to know what you thought she liked," I said, intrigued. He poured himself a drink.

"I... you know, stuck a finger in her..." he pulled in his lips and pushed them out quickly, making a popping sound, while making a circular motion in the air with his pointer finger.

I stalked closer to him, captivated. "In her what?" He took a sip of his drink.

18

"You know, her..." he pointed towards my behind.

I felt my mouth drop in shock. "You put your finger in her butt!" I exclaimed.

"Yeah," he said, shrugging.

"What kind of girl likes that?" I asked, horrified. He grinned.

"A lot of them."

I swiftly turned around to go back to cutting my limes.

"You know, had you taken her number, you could have avoided this whole mess. You would have seen it pop up when you were putting it in your phone."

"Whatever," he simply replied.

"So... you didn't finish?" I asked.

"Oh, I finished. Just by myself," he said as he started making a drink for a customer who had just arrived.

"You're vile," I said, now attending to another customer.

"Oh, please, everyone masturbates. I hate when girls pretend that they don't. Don't be one of those girls. It's perfectly natural. Nothing to be ashamed of."

"You're such a dick," I said, shaking my head and disregarding his statement.

He didn't say anything as we were serving, but as soon as our customers took their drinks to a table, he turned around and said, "I'm not a dick, by the way. I'm honest. I've never told a girl I was looking for anything I wasn't, and anyone who has been with me knew beforehand what I was interested in. And, more importantly, what I wasn't interested in. It turns out; I just have a bad memory."

Spring was coming, the weather was getting nice out, and it got rather busy for a Friday night. "I don't see why girls like you so much."

He grinned. "You don't, huh? I'm very charming and quite skilled, if you know what I mean."

I shot him a fake smile as I counted the register.

"You don't believe me?" He asked, leaning up against the soda tap. "I bet you twenty bucks I can get you wet in three seconds."

I let out a cynical laugh and turned around, inching towards him.

"You're so sure of that?" I said, staring into his eyes.

"Yeah, I am," he confidently replied.

I retrieved the twenty from my pocket I had taken from him earlier. We made stupid bets like this all the time. It entertained us and made the night go by a little faster. My arm brushed against his as I put it on the bar behind him.

He gazed into my eyes and slowly started counting out loud.

"One... two..." I'm not going to lie; with my eyes deeply in his, stories about his sexual encounters floating through my head, I did begin to lose myself in fantasy. Did he have some sort of mind manipulation powers over females, like the girls had said? I could feel my heart start to race in anticipation of what he was about to do. "Three," he concluded as he sprayed me with the water tap.

I jumped back in shock, now looking at my soaked t-shirt. He took the twenty from the bar and laughed. "Told you I could get you wet."

"That's not fair!" I exclaimed and grabbed the soda gun and shot him back.

"Hey, I shot you with water; that's soda!" He argued. I started walking towards him with my arm raised to take my money back. He slowly inched away from me until he was at the end of the bar. Now leaning against the bar, unable to get any further, he lifted the money above his head. He was at least a good foot taller than me, so retrieving the twenty was harder than I anticipated. "I said I could get you wet, and I did – it's mine. Fair and square."

Standing between his legs with my hand on his thigh, I reached up to try to grab the money he was holding up. Then, on my tippy toes, with my cheek pressed against his, I whispered in his ear, "I bet I can get you *aroused* in three seconds."

He looked down at me. Our eyes now locked, his lips so close to mine I could feel his breath on me, and said: "Too late, I already am. That's another superhero ability I have; I'm *always* aroused."

I jumped up a little, snatched the money out of his hand, and escaped back to the register to continue counting.

"A regular superhero over here," I said while counting. "What's your secret identity? A douchebag?" One thing that I always loved about James was how comfortable I was talking to him. There wasn't much I couldn't say to him; he didn't offend easily.

"No, the Biggest Asshole. Just look at your phone," he said. I put the money from the register in an envelope and handed it to him. He took the cash out and calculated my share. Unlike the other bartenders, he paid me ten percent of whatever the bar brought in. That was the agreement when he made me the manager two years before. So, when the bar did good, like that Friday night in particular, I did great. It was hard to leave, and the fact that we had such a good relationship made it that much harder.

I met Mia the next day for brunch. The little mom-and-pop-owned pub located conveniently between our apartments was a place we went to often. Low key, no one was ever too dressed up, and it was relatively cheap compared to the other restaurants in the area. It had high-top tables, the bar lit up with Christmas-type lights, and nineties alternative music blasting no matter what the time.

Pushing around the remains of my salad, I couldn't get the conversation I had with James out of my head.

"Have you ever had a guy put a finger in your, you know...?" As I made a circular motion with my pointer finger and made the same popping sound that he had. She looked up from her phone.

"In my what?"

"You know, your..." I repeated, jerking my head towards my behind.

"My ass?" She asked as if she were completing a sentence on a gameshow.

"Yeah, your ass."

"Like randomly?" She asked, taking another mouthful of food.

"No, not randomly, like in the middle of sex."

She swallowed her bite of food and took a sip of her drink. "I mean yeah, like if he was going down on me, or doggie style." As if a lightbulb went off in her mind, Mia said with a shocked look on her face, "Oh my god, did Evan do it for the first time? The first time it happens, it's always kinda weird, especially if you aren't expecting it."

"No, I was talking to James, and...." She cut me off.

"Okay, I'm going to stop you right there. That's your first problem; never talk to *James* about sex!" She said.

"You think he's cute?" I asked, resting my chin in the

palm of my hand and leaning on the table.

"Hell yeah, he's fine as fuck. But talking to him about sex is like joining the Olympics, without ever going to the gym in your life," she laughed.

"Rob looks just like him, and you think he's ugly," I said.

"Rob is just a dick. If I saw him on the street and didn't know him, I'd probably think he was cute. But I do know him – too much. James, without a doubt, has a better personality," she reasoned.

"Do you think I am a prude?" I asked.

"A prude? No – you've just been with a few guys. What is the craziest thing you've ever done in bed?" She asked.

"I mean, Evan has never worn a diaper, if that's what you're asking," I said, laughing. I thought for a minute. What was the craziest thing I have ever done?

"Oh!" I said, pointing at her, remembering one event. "He tied me up once!"

She smiled and raised her eyebrows, trying her best to look impressed, but plainly was not.

"See, you're not a prude!" She agreed.

"But, he did accidentally tie my legs together," I admitted. She almost spit her drink out, holding back laughter. "And he made the knot so tight; it took him a while to undo it." She swallowed the liquid in her mouth so as not to choke on it.

"You got a real boy scout over there," she joked.

When Evan and I did have sex, it was good; at least I thought it was. Suddenly I felt like there was this entire world of sex I didn't know – I felt so inexperienced. I silently wondered if I was marrying Evan for the right reasons. I had been so wrapped up in my life plan; I had never questioned things like our sex life. It had never been an important factor for me before. Why was I examining it now? I changed the subject and went back to my drink.

Chapter Three

"I cannot believe you two will be married in six months! You must be so excited!" Evan's mother said to me later during an early dinner with his parents.

I tried to hide a yawn with my hand as I looked up from my fruit salad.

"I go for my second fitting for my dress Friday," I said.

"That you can do on Friday, huh?" Evan rudely quipped.

"Yes, before work," I said without looking at him.

Evan's parents could sense the tension. Heck, the table next to us could probably feel it also.

"Evan, do you know how stressful it is to be a bride?" His mother defended me.

His mother and I had become close throughout the years. She was much younger than my mother, with dark hair and light eyes. Always well put together and very in shape. His father was a successful attorney, and she was a doctor. Evan was used to growing up with money, so it was difficult for him to understand how hard I worked for mine.

Evan put his fork down and looked up at her. "You know how stressful it is to be the fiancé of a bartender? Never around on the weekends, holidays, or special events."

"Evan is getting an award on Friday – highest-ranking salesman of the year," I said, trying my hardest to sound impressed.

"And my fiancé can't even come with me," he said.

"I'll go with you," his mother offered.

"Yes, that's exactly what I want, my mommy to come with me."

"Don't talk to your mother that way!" His father interjected. Evan just looked back down at his food.

"Where is your bachelorette party?" His mother asked me, changing the subject.

"New Orleans in July. We're celebrating my thirtieth there also. Kill two birds with one stone."

I couldn't wait to get away already. His mother was right; planning a wedding was extremely stressful, and it consumed all of my free time.

After dinner, Evan and I walked back to our apartment. As I stood in front of the mirror refreshing my make-up, I asked Evan what his plans for the night were.

"I'm going to a club with the guys," he said with an attitude.

"Why don't you guys stop by the bar to pre-game?" I suggested, trying to lighten the mood.

Although he said he might stop in, there was no sight of Evan and his friends by the time the last call rolled around.

When I returned home, he was already sleeping. Attempting to make up for the friction in our relationship lately, I changed into a sexy nightgown and slowly crawled on him, kissing his neck to wake him up. As his eyes slowly started opening, he put his hands on my waist and lifted me off him.

"I'm too tired," he mumbled.

I rolled over to face him. "You didn't come to the bar tonight," I said.

He turned his head to look at me. "I did. You were too enthralled with James to notice. You know how embarrassing that was in front of my friends?" He replied.

"What? That's ridiculous. James and I just work together," I answered.

"Yeah, you work *real* close together. I saw the way he put his hand on your waist to get past you. You didn't even flinch, as if that were just normal behavior for the two of you."

"Are you kidding me?" I began. "You're jealous of James? Of all people – James? The number one 'man whore' of *all* man whores?"

"No, I'm not jealous of him. It was disrespectful," he said. That hadn't been the first time he had something to say about my relationship with James.

"There isn't that much room behind the bar. So sometimes we do have to make contact to get past each other," I tried explaining.

"Okay," he said, rolling his eyes. "I'm tired, and I'm going back to sleep."

Things had been getting heated between Evan and me for a few months already, but I was confident that it would get better once we married. Unfortunately, his mom was right, and this was an extremely stressful time for both of us.

When Friday came around, I was lugging shopping bags up the steps. We lived on the second floor of an apartment building, and it didn't help out that James had asked me to pick up two bottles of Tito's because we were almost out before our alcohol delivery came. Out of breath, I put the food away and grabbed a yogurt, and ate it as fast as I could. I looked at my watch; it was four fifteen. I had fifteen minutes to make it to my dress fitting and then get to work.

"You lost an inch!" The girl said, looking at the tape measure as I stared at myself in the mirror. Every time I went to get sized, the dress seemed to get more and more beautiful.

"I've been trying," I admitted. "But I can tell you I am going to devour that wedding cake, so make sure you leave some room for that!"

"You look gorgeous," she commented.

I smiled, still looking at myself in the mirror. It was such a shame you only got to wear a dress like that one night of your life.

"Thank you. I almost don't want to take it off!" I confessed as she unzipped the back. I put my clothes back on and made my way to the bar. I was about two blocks in when I realized I had left the vodka at home. In a panic, I hailed a cab. I instructed him to leave the meter running and flew up the stairs, keys in hand. I put the key in the door, but it wasn't opening. I started frantically trying every key, afraid I was now going to be late for work. I paused for a moment to analyze every key, when suddenly I heard shuffling in the apartment. I knocked on the door loudly.

"Evan? Are you home? Open the door; I need to get something."

A few seconds later, I heard the door unbolt, and he stood in front of me. I rushed past him to the kitchen to grab the bottles. "Why did you bolt the door?" I asked.

"Force of habit," he replied. I grabbed the bottles of alcohol and went to make my way out when the time suddenly occurred to me.

"Why are you home so early?" I asked.

"They let us out early because of the event tonight. I was playing a video game, I didn't hear you trying to get in," he said, his voice cracking a bit.

I looked at the TV that the game system was hooked up to, and it was off. Looking him up and down, I noticed he was sweating; his face flushed, and he didn't have a shirt on. My eyes started scanning the room. There was a pocketbook on the couch that hadn't belonged to me.

"Is someone here?" I asked, afraid to hear his answer. He didn't say anything as I made my way towards the bedroom. As I got closer, he desperately said: "Don't go in there!"

I slowly turned around to face him, staring at him in disbelief. I was nervous and sick to my stomach at the same time. Finally, I lifted my hand and knocked on the door behind me.

"Excuse me, slut in my bedroom?" I announced. "I am about to enter; please be dressed to avoid any further embarrassment."

As I turned and pushed open the bedroom door, he was pleading with me to stop. When the door opened, there she stood. She was tall, with dark curly hair, and her shirt on inside out, as if she just threw it over her head.

"I didn't know he had a girlfriend," she defensively said.

"Oh, I'm not his girlfriend; I'm his fiancé," I said, holding up my left hand flashing my engagement ring. "I'm the girl in the picture with him right there, right next to the bed you were just on," I continued, pointing at the night table. It made me even angrier that she had the nerve to lie to me about it.

"Amber, please..." he began.

"Shut up!" I was now screaming. "*This* is what you cheat on me with!? She isn't even pretty!"

"Hey, fuck you," she said. I quickly spun around to face her.

"No fuck you!" I screamed. "You better shut your mouth before I bash your face through that wall!"

Evan started approaching me; his hands held out in a submissive form. "Amber, please..."

I took my ring off and threw it at him. I quickly rushed into the kitchen to get the alcohol.

"I don't have time for this. I'm going to work," I said calmly. "When I get back, you both better be gone, along with your things."

"I can explain," he argued.

"There's nothing to explain. We're over," I said and ran down the stairs.

Fortunately, the cab was still waiting for me. I was relatively calm during the short drive, but when I walked into the bar, James looked up and smiled at me as I passed the alcohol to Kaitlyn over the bar. All of a sudden, I could feel the tears welling up in my eyes. I hurried out the back door to the yard and lit a cigarette. I was sick to my stomach. It sank in what I had just witnessed in my apartment. Now, crying hysterically, I sat on the cold floor and smoked my cigarette. The more I tried to calm myself down, the faster the tears were falling. I lit a second cigarette. My hands were shaking, and I couldn't stop my heart from racing.

After a few minutes, I heard the door open, and James came out. He lit a cigarette and slowly started walking towards me.

"Are you okay?" He asked, now standing over me.

I nodded. "I'm fine. I just need a minute. I'll be right in; I'm sorry I'm late."

"What's wrong?" He asked.

"Nothing," I said, my voice trembling as I was trying to hold back tears.

He sat down on the concrete next to me. We both sat quietly, smoking our cigarettes. It wasn't long before he broke the silence. "Do you want to talk about it?"

I sat for a few seconds, trying to formulate the words.

"I forgot the Tito's. I had to go back to my apartment," I said.

He put his hand on my knee. "It's not a big deal. You were like ten minutes late. Are you that afraid of me?" He asked, laughing.

"Evan was home, and he was with a girl – in *my* bedroom!"

His mouth dropped. He took his hand off my knee and placed it on his forehead like he didn't know what to say. Then he stood up and took his phone out of his pocket.

"I'm going to call Bruce to fill in. Go home. It would be best if you weren't working like this," he said, now scrolling through his phone for Bruce's number.

"No, I can't go home; I don't want to see him. I'm fine. I just need a second...."

"You're not fine," he argued. He started talking on the phone. "Hey, I know it's last minute, but can you come work today? Something came up; bring your brother too."

He hung up the phone and walked back towards me, kneeling in front of me.

"They'll be here in twenty minutes. We'll go out. Get drunk somewhere. You don't have to go home, but you definitely cannot get behind that bar tonight."

We sat in silence as we waited for Bruce and Jason to arrive. I didn't even know what I was feeling. In that moment, I was more embarrassed than anything else now that James knew Evan cheated on me. I didn't know why I even cared what he thought, but I did. I felt inconvenienced that I now had to figure out how to cancel a wedding. I was confused and questioning myself as to why I wasn't even hurting over the fact that Evan was with another girl. When Bruce and Jason showed up, James and I walked to a bar a few blocks away. I could barely even remember the walk; I was in such a daze. When we sat at the bar, he ordered two double Jameson's. We drank them pretty fast, and the second round was already coming. Finally, after three doubles, I was numb and ready to start the conversation.

"I'm sorry I dragged you into this," I said.

The bartender came over and handed us menus.

"Nah, you're fine. It's been a while since I've been out on a Friday night, it was long overdue," he rationalized.

32

"You know what I want?" I asked him. He twisted his head, waiting for my request. I shifted my eyes back to the bartender. "I want fries. With cheese, a lot of cheese. And onion rings. You know what, an order of jalapeno poppers too!"

He let out a breath and looked at me, blinking rapidly. "That's quite a meal. I'll just have a burger, please," he ordered.

I turned my barstool to face him, placing my foot on his stool.

"Don't you dare judge me; I haven't eaten a carb in a year," I said. He laughed.

"I'm not judging you. There's nothing better than a girl who's not afraid to eat," he said. "See, now you can eat like a human again. And just think of all that money you'll have in your account now that you don't have to pay for a wedding!"

"You know, you're probably the smartest person I know. Who needs to be tied down in a relationship? You can do whatever you want, whenever you want, without hurting anyone. I wish I were a man sometimes," I admitted.

"You don't need to be a man not to be tied down," he said.

The food came, and I took a fry and put it in my mouth. "Oh my god, this is heaven!" I exclaimed, now picking up a fry and putting it in his mouth. "Try it."

He took the fry in his mouth and, after swallowing, said: "Yeah, tastes like a French fry."

After a few more drinks, we were heavily in conversation.

"You know what your problem is?" He slurred. I

leaned in as if he were just about to relay the secret of the universe to me. "You're too much of a planner; you never just let loose and see what happens. Live a little! Be spontaneous, have a one-night stand. Or even better, rebound sex – works every time. Get a guy, or girl if that's your thing – better looking than him and go to town with them. Do things you always wanted to do but were too embarrassed. Things you didn't do with Evan. I'm telling you; sex is a lot different when you don't have to wake up next to him every morning." He started looking around the room. "What about those guys over there?" He asked, pointing at a group of athletic-looking guys, in their thirties. "Any of those guys do it for you?"

I examined the men. "The guy in the red is kind of cute," I said.

He turned around in his chair to get a better look at the guys.

"Really?" He said, sounding unimpressed with my choice. "The one in the red? Doesn't seem to be your type."

"How do you know my type?" I asked.

"Well, I mean – Evan," he said.

"Evan was never my type. He is just a good guy, or at least I thought he was. I like the jock-looking guys. The ones who look like real assholes," I said.

"Okay, well, I'm sitting here with you, so they may think we're together. I'll go to the bathroom, and you try to get eye contact with him. Once the conversation starts, say I am your brother," he instructed. "I'll play along."

He disappeared to go to the bathroom, and I did as he suggested. Once I had made eye contact, I smiled, and he came over to the bar next to me to order a drink.

"Is this seat taken?" He asked, patting James' seat.

"Yes, but it's just my brother. You can sit; he won't mind," I responded.

"I'm Joey," he introduced himself.

"I'm Amber."

"That's a beautiful name," he said, now taking a sip of his drink.

"Thanks," I gushed, looking down at the plates of food in front of me.

"That's a lot of food," he remarked, also looking down at the plates.

"When I do something, I go all the way," I flirtatiously responded. He smiled and bit his bottom lip. A dimple emerged in his cheek. James came back from the bathroom, and Joey stood to give him back his seat.

"No, it's fine, I'd rather stand," he said, now coming to the left of me and ordering us another round of drinks. I had never really been in a public setting with James before, and he was drunker than I had ever seen him.

He took his drink, nodded at Joey then looked at me.

"You have something on your mouth," he said.

"I do?" I asked, trying to feel for it. He moved in closer and gently put his finger on my bottom lip to wipe away whatever was on it.

"Cheese," he said, showing me the remnants on his finger. Joey had an expression of shock on his face. I froze, realizing that if he were my brother, that would be pretty strange the way his finger laid on my bottom lip. I pulled away and turned back to Joey. "It was nice meeting you, Amber," he said as he got up to walk back over to his friends. James went back into his seat.

"What happened?" He asked, clueless.

"I said you were my brother, remember?" I laughed.

He didn't get it at first, but then it occurred to him.

"Oh shit, my bad. Sorry," he said.

"It's okay," I reassured him. "Not like I am going to sleep with someone tonight anyway."

Now back with his friends, Joey, obviously talking about us, had all his friends staring. James turned around and noticed it also. "Let's get out of here," he said, signaling to the bartender for the check. "Want to go to a club?" He asked as we were walking out. I looked down at my watch. It wasn't even midnight yet.

"Sure."

We went to a club downtown and continued our drinking fest. The place was packed. With the DJ playing, lights flashing, you could barely walk through the dance floor. People were drenched in sweat. It was weird being out with James and seeing how he was in public. He had such a way with the girls; they all loved him. Buying drinks for everyone, no one even cared if I was his sister or girlfriend; they just wanted him. He was definitely the life of the party, hilarious and a lot of fun to hang out with.

It almost became a competition with the girls about who would be the one to go home with him, as they were all trying their best to impress him. He didn't seem phased, though; he was more focused on me. We hung out by the bar and talked and danced. He suggested we play a drinking game and take a shot every time I mentioned Evan. Needless to say, we were hammered by two a.m.

"I have a favor to ask you," I began. "I have no idea if Evan...."

"Shots," he chimed in, ordering two more at Evan's name.

I took the shot and continued. "I have no idea if that

asshole I was supposed to marry is going to be at my apartment. Can I stay by you tonight?"

He seemed a little surprised at first but then said, "Sure, I have an extra bedroom." So, we remained at the club for another half an hour before we started heading back to his place.

Chapter Four

He had a great apartment. A huge living room with a fantastic view of the city. Black leather couches and an enormous TV that covered the entire wall. His coffee table was a fish tank that had actual fish swimming around. I sat on the sofa smiling at the fish as he disappeared into the bedroom. He came back with two glasses of Jameson and a t-shirt with a pair of boxer briefs for me to sleep in tucked under his arm. "They're relaxing, right? Watching them?" He remarked as he sat next to me, eyes fixated on the tank.

"You have a bar in your bedroom?" I asked.

"Something like that," he replied, handing me a glass. I took a sip of the drink then sat it down on the coffee table. Laying down, I rested my head in his lap, looking up at him. "You had to see how ugly this girl was," I said.

He looked down at me. "Don't say his name – I can't handle another shot," he warned. "Was she really ugly, or are you just being dramatic because you're mad?"

I sat back up, now sitting on my knees on the couch facing him. I thought about it for a second.

"I'm probably exaggerating a bit, but she definitely wasn't all that," I admitted. I placed the t-shirt he gave me down on the couch and took mine off. He sat there staring at me, and his mouth hung a little; shocked, I guessed that I was changing in front of him.

"Look at me," I said, sitting in front of him in only a blue lace bra and my jeans.

"Are you kidding me? I couldn't look at anything else if I tried," he said, without shifting his gaze.

"Do you think I'm hot? You can be honest," I asked.

He paused for a second, still enthralled by my chest. "Incredibly hot," he muttered, almost under his breath.

"So rebound sex, huh? You think that will work?" I said.

"Yes, rebound sex," he reiterated, nodding. I leaned in closer to him and kissed him on the lips. He was surprised at first but placed his drink down on the table and kissed me back gently. He ran his hands from my waist, slowly up my arms, to my shoulders, and pushed me back lightly.

"I didn't mean with me," he stated. I looked down at my chest mortified as if it had just occurred to me that I was only in my bra. As my eyes shifted back up towards him, he was leaning back towards me, his lips reattaching to mine as if he couldn't control himself. "Although it's not a horrible idea," he mumbled, not taking his lips off mine. I climbed on top of him, my legs around his waist, pulling him closer to me by the back of his neck and rubbing myself on him. I could feel him getting turned on against me. He put his hands on my hips, guiding me back and forth on him. Feeling him aroused under his jeans turned me on more than I would have thought. I started kissing his neck as he ran his hands around my behind, now pulling me harder into him.

"You like when girls take charge?" I whispered in his ear.

He slowly ran his hands up my body to my bra straps and pulled them down at the same time, exposing my breasts. Then, as he started kissing them, he said, "I do, but right now, I think you need someone to take charge."

He lifted me off him and laid me down on my back. Enthusiastically kissing my body, from my neck, down my breasts, and then to my belly button where his lips remained gently sucking as he unzipped my jeans. He wrestled them off me, not moving his attention away from my torso. As he was focused on my belly button, his fingers caressed me between my legs as he slid my panties to the side and slipped two in me.

I was more turned on in that moment than I had been in years, and all I could picture was his mouth there. He didn't go there immediately, though, as if he were teasing me. Finally, when I couldn't take it anymore, I pushed his head down, directing his lips between my legs. His fingers stayed in me as he continued, his left hand running up and down my body. It had been so long since a man got me that excited, so it was no surprise that it didn't take very long for me to orgasm.

He pushed himself up, now on his knees, and took his shirt off, his six-pack glistening in the dim lights. Damn, I suddenly realized just how hot he was. He had a tattoo of a dog tag that wrapped around his neck and hung down his chest with a number sketched on it. By far the hottest guy I had ever been with, he was utterly out of my league. He crawled on top of me and continued kissing me vehemently as I unzipped his jeans and reached my hand in. The rumors were correct; he was tremendous. I stroked him as he reached into his back pocket and pulled out his wallet. He shuffled through it quickly, took out a condom, and then flung the wallet on the floor. I couldn't get his pants off fast enough. I gasped at his size as he entered me.

He paused for a second, motionless inside of me. "You okay?" He asked. "You want me to go slow?"

I shook my head, pulling him deeper into me. Suddenly I needed him; I needed to feel him, see for myself what everyone was talking about. "No," I moaned.

"I've thought about this for a long time," he grumbled in my ear. I pulled him into me as he quickened his pace. Thrusting himself inside me passionately as if we both realized in that second, we had been longing for each other for years.

"Just this once," I said, still kissing him and running my fingers through his hair.

"One and done," he agreed. "Turn over."

He pushed himself up and backed up, so I could turn around. As my hand grabbed the couch cushion, he pulled me up into him, forcing me to my knees. As he penetrated me from behind, I felt his right hand go from my breasts and down my stomach, until his fingers were massaging me between my legs simultaneously. His left hand was holding me steadily up by my waist. Suddenly I felt very self-conscious that I looked fat in that position and tried to cover my stomach with my arms as I tensed up, fearing falling off the couch.

I felt his lips work their way from the back of my shoulder, up to my neck, and to my ear. His facial hair brushing lightly against my neck, I reached behind and held onto the back of his neck for support.

"Relax," he whispered in my ear. "I got you." I eased up and rested the back of my head against his chest and closed my eyes, enjoying every moment as my body uncontrollably responded to his every touch.

It didn't take longer than twenty minutes, but when we got finished, I felt a sense of relief I hadn't had in years, maybe ever.

I woke up to the sun blaring in my eyes, in my bra and panties – my body halfway hanging off the couch. James was passed out on the floor. The second I opened my eyes, I felt the throbbing in my head. As I grabbed the t-shirt he had given me the night before and pulled it over my head, he slowly started to push himself up, now sitting and putting on his boxer briefs. He rested his head in his hands, rubbing his temples. He peered up at me through his fingers. "You're not gonna sue me, are you?" He asked.

I stood up to stretch my body and suddenly felt dizzy.

"Get over yourself. This isn't corporate America, and I made the first move on you."

He started moving his neck from side to side, clearly hungover as well.

"Two excellent points," he said.

"Have you ever heard of room darkening blinds?" I asked.

"I don't typically sleep in the living room," he replied.

"Tell me you have a coffee machine," I said. He pointed towards the kitchen. As I made my way there, he added,

"Pods are in the drawer under it."

I rummaged through the cabinet to find a mug. He walked in a few seconds later and handed me a bottle of Motrin as he swallowed his without a drink. He sat down at the table. I placed the cup of coffee in front of him and started making another. He took a sip of his coffee and looked up at me. "How do you feel?" He asked.

"Despite the massive hangover, surprisingly a little better," I admitted, sitting down across from him.

He smiled. "Glad I can help."

"We can't tell anybody about this!" I said.

He chuckled. "Who am I going to tell?"

My head rested on my hand as I held it up with my elbow on the table. We sat in silence while we drank our coffee. After I finished it, I put the cup in the sink and went to retrieve my clothes.

"It's been a while since I've done the walk of shame," I said, zipping up my jeans. He came over to me and ran his fingers through my hair to help it from looking disheveled.

"You look fine," he assured me.

"So, I guess I'll see you later," I awkwardly said, making my way to the door.

"Yeah, see you later," he repeated.

He only lived two blocks away from me, but the walk seemed like a mile. I couldn't help but feel like everyone was looking at me, knowing where I was and who I was with.

When I walked into my apartment, I was startled to see Evan sitting on the couch.

"Long night, huh?" He said.

"What are you still doing here?" I asked, not looking at him and heading towards the bedroom.

"Stop," he pleaded, approaching me. "Let's talk about this."

"There's nothing to talk about," I simply said. He tried to put his arms around my waist as I quickly pulled back from him. "Don't touch me!"

"We already put a down payment on a hall!" He argued.

I looked at him appalled. "Are you kidding me? That's what you're worried about, the down payment? How about the fact you cheated on me? The humiliation, the disgust I have for you...."

"No one needs to know. It was a stupid thing to do; I know it was. I love you, I was just really stressed, and she was easy, and...." I cut him off.

"Just shut up; you don't love me. And in my own fucking bed!"

He sat back down on the couch, "Look, you quite clearly got screwed last night. Do you feel better now? We're even. Let's just move past this, please! I'm sorry...."

I shook my head in revulsion and started back towards the door to leave. "I'm serious, Evan; I want you gone by the time I get back!" I said, slamming the door.

I hailed a cab and texted Mia that I was on the way to her apartment. When she opened the door, she looked like she had just woken up. "What time is it?" She asked.

"Noon," I replied, walking in.

Unlike me, who lived on the second floor, she lived on the first. Mia's apartment was a lot nicer than mine, despite it being a studio. She had all new appliances and high-end radiators, unlike the old, rotted ones I had in my apartment. She hated living on the first floor because she said the kids walking upstairs would wake her up. She was a neat freak, and her place was always so clean. She had real leather sofas and a decent sized TV rested on top of a bookshelf. Her couch opened to a queen-size bed at the press of a button, not the old pull-out types. Her kitchen was attached but appeared a lot bigger than it was and had enough space for a full-size table and four chairs.

"What are you doing up so early?" She asked. As I sat on her couch that was now open to a bed, tears started rolling down my face. "What's wrong? Are you okay?" She sat down next to me, putting her arm around me.

"He cheated on me – last night. I had to go back to the house, and he had a girl there. An *ugly* girl at that, in my bedroom."

She sat stunned for a second. She opened her mouth as if she were going to say something, but nothing came out. Instead, she pulled me in closer to her.

"The wedding is off," I said, laying my head on her shoulder. She nodded in acknowledgment but didn't say anything. She sat with me for a while, then got up to make a cup of coffee.

"You want one?"

I just shook my head no.

"So, now what?" She asked.

"I told him to leave. He is still there now, that's why I came here. I need to work tonight; I'll need to use your shower if that's okay."

"Of course, you can use my shower. Did you work last night? After all this?" She asked.

"No," I said. "I left work. I didn't come home this morning until just before I came here. He was supposed to be gone."

"Where were you all night?" She asked with a

questioning look in her eyes. I looked down.

"Yeah, I'll take a cup of coffee," I said, changing the subject. She went into the kitchen, made me a cup, handed it to me, and then sat back down next to me.

"Where were you?" She asked again.

I looked up at her. She stared at me anxiously, waiting for an answer. I let out a sigh and answered reluctantly: "I was with James." Her mouth dropped, and her eyebrows raised.

"James? Rob's brother James? Your boss James? *That* James?" She asked.

I just nodded. She leaned in closer to me. "Did you sleep with him?"

I nodded again. She jumped up from the couch. "Are you insane? You don't shit where you eat! He's your boss, Amber. Are you nuts?"

"Oh my God, with this 'boss' thing... we're bartenders, and he happens to own the bar. It's not a real company; I don't get an actual paycheck with his signature on it," I defended myself.

"He can fire you. That's as real as it gets," she said.

I rested my head back in my hands. "He's not going to fire me, Mia. It's James, and sex is just another day to him. It's like breathing."

Realizing nothing she could say could take back what happened, she sat back down on the couch. "So, are the rumors true?" She asked, now very curious. I rolled my eyes. "Oh no, no – you cannot blurt out that you slept with James and not address every single story we heard about him!"

I turned my body to face her. "You can't tell anybody!" I started.

"I swear, I would never," she insisted.

"He's enormous and amazingly talented. That's all I can confirm. He didn't do anything too weird or freaky. There was no video camera. He didn't ask me to do anything I didn't want to do – and I made the first move on him."

She started to laugh. "You hoe! Well, he certainly is an upgrade from Evan."

"It was just a one-time thing," I said. "It's never going to happen again."

She got up and went back to the kitchen and came back with two cherry danishes.

"Sure it isn't," she said, handing me one.

"What are you talking about? We've been working together for almost five years; you think I can't control myself around him?" I asked.

"Obviously not," she said, still laughing. I stayed at her place and got ready for work. She gave me an extra key should I have to go back there again.

When James walked in, I was entertaining a customer, so he caught me off guard when I turned around to go to the register, and he was right behind me. Startled, I jumped back a bit. "You okay?" He asked.

"Yeah, I'm good," I said as I quickly brushed past him to the register. Suddenly, it clicked that I had sex with him the night before, and all I could envision was him on top of me, kissing me, running his hands down my body. I felt flushed in the face, silently praying I wasn't blushing.

I tried to keep my distance from him all night. Anytime he said something, all I could hear was him whispering in my ear. Anytime his hand touched anything near me, I saw it on my body. I didn't dare look at his lips. He seemed to be having the same problem as he was also different; he was not very talkative and stand-offish. When he spoke, it was in a serious tone, not flirtatious at all. So many emotions fluttered through my head. I went from being embarrassed to turned on by the previous night's memories and then paranoid he regretted it.

When it slowed down around three a.m., I poured myself a vodka soda and stood in the corner, guzzling it down. My heart was beating so fast as I was trying to process what had just happened in the past twenty-four hours. When I finished my drink, I poured myself another. As I turned around, drink in hand, James was getting change from the register and looking over at me. We made eye contact. We looked at each other for what seemed to be an eternity, and he smiled slightly. I smiled back and immediately looked down at my glass.

He finished with his customer, sauntered his way over to me, and reached for a bottle of Jameson. "Good idea, the hair of the dog," he said. It was the first time all night either one of us acknowledged anything had happened the night before. We didn't speak until Kaitlyn left, and we were alone closing up.

As I was by the register, counting out the money, my back to him – I could hear him making another drink.

"Are we good?" He asked nervously.

I turned and looked at him as he was leaning against the bar. I smiled. "Yeah, we're good," I said, looking around the counter. "Where are the envelopes?"

He came up behind me and extended his arm past me to get the envelopes, his arm brushing up against mine. My body stiffened as I slowly turned around to face him. Our eyes met again, and he held up the box of envelopes without turning his gaze. I could see the piece of his tattoo sticking out of his t-shirt, and all I could imagine was stripping his shirt off. Without blinking or saying another word, we were uncontrollably leaning into each other. I was on my tippy toes, pulling him into me as I could taste the whiskey on his tongue. He put his hands around my waist and pulled me closer to him, feeling his body up against mine. I pulled away for a second.

"We said one night."

He pulled back also, still staring into my eyes.

"Right, once," he agreed.

Neither of us moved. We both just stood there staring at each other until we were suddenly kissing again. He was such a good kisser that it was hard to resist him. He pulled his lips off mine, but his mouth was so close that they were still practically touching.

"One can make the argument we didn't specify one time or one day." He looked at his watch. "Technically, we're still within twenty-four hours."

That was all he had to say. Placing his hands back on my waist sent shivers down my body. No man had ever turned me on like he had. We couldn't take our hands off each other. The following day, I woke up next to him in his bed.

I slowly sat up in his bed, taking in my surroundings as my fingers grazed the soft red satin sheets under me. The bed was king-size and lifted higher than a standard bed with a black dresser and matching nightstand. He had a similar TV hanging on the wall like his living room. There was a bar in the corner containing full bottles of vodka, gin, tequila, whiskey, mixers, and glasses. A matching black leather loveseat with red velvet throw pillows and a round glass coffee table sat under the window. With expensive-looking paintings hanging on the walls, all sex-themed, it seemed more like a lounge than a bedroom.

James sat up and rubbed his eyes. "This is so not what I pictured your room to look like," I commented. He looked over at me.

"Oh no? What did you picture?" He asked.

"I don't know. I guess I never thought about it," I confessed.

He smiled. "Well, you're obviously thinking about it now, so what's so shocking? Is it the bar?" He asked, laughing.

"No, I don't know. I'd take you for a blue guy. Maybe gray. Sports memorabilia like at the bar. It's not a bad thing; it's a nice room. I just didn't expect it. I guess I have just never seen you in red, so I didn't take you as a red type of guy." He stared at me intensely.

"A red type of guy? I didn't know red was a type," he said as he slipped on his boxer briefs and stood up. "You don't find red to be sexy?"

"Yes, red is sexy," I admitted.

"So, it's me you don't find to be sexy?" He asked.

"I didn't say that! I just mean...." He started laughing and held out his hand to help me out of bed. "Come here."

"Where are you taking me?" I asked, pulling back a little.

"I wanna show you something," he said, still smiling. I took his hand and followed his lead past the living room to another door that was shut. As he began to open it, I wasn't sure what to expect. After hearing all the rumors about him, all I could envision was a sex swing in the middle of the room, with video cameras set up, maybe some sex toys. Hesitant, I dropped my hand from his and stood in the doorway, trying not to look in.

He raised his eyebrows. "What are you so afraid of? What do you think is in here?"

"I don't know. What *is* in there?" I asked.

He pulled me by the waist with both his hands. "Come look." There I stood in a bedroom, exactly as I described—blue bedsheets with a gray comforter and sports collectibles on the walls.

"What is this?" I asked.

"My bedroom."

"So, wait – you have a sex room?" I asked.

"No, it's not a 'sex room'," he said with air quotes. "It's an entertaining room."

"An entertaining room? Do you entertain men in there?" I asked, placing my hands on my hips.

"No," he laughed.

"So, then it's a sex room," I insisted.

"No, it's not. It's just a room that I...." as he was trying to find the right word, I chimed in.

"Do you ever have sex with girls in this room?" I asked, pointing at his bed.

"No."

"Why not?"

"I don't know. I don't want my room smelling like a chick's perfume."

"No girl ever wanted to have sex in here?" I asked. He grinned as he pushed me back past the doorway and shut the door behind him.

"No girl ever questioned that room or called me out on not being what they expected," he said. "Gotta be honest,

I'm not sure if I should be impressed or scared at how well you know me."

"Don't flatter yourself. Up until yesterday, I didn't even think I was attracted to you," I said as I went back to the 'entertaining room' to gather my clothes.

"And now you do think you're attracted to me?" He shot back. I ignored his question and threw my clothes back on. It was true, suddenly after all this time I found myself extremely attracted to him. I smirked as I headed towards the door.

"Bye, James," I said, winking at him, still refusing to answer his question. He smiled back as his teeth clamped his bottom lip.

"Bye, Amber."

Chapter Five

The following week was excruciating. I had thought planning a wedding was stressful, but it was even more traumatic to cancel one. Every place I called wanted to know what happened. By the third phone call, I angrily said he had died. It was humiliating to tell people he cheated on me. His mother called me about six times, begging me to reconsider. After that, I wanted nothing to do with Evan ever again; I didn't even want to hear his name.

By the next Friday night, things were back to normal between James and me behind the bar. It wasn't weird, no tension, back to our regular flirty banter. The only difference from the week before was the three guys lingering around after the last call. They were drinking their drinks so slowly, James finally told them they had to leave, that we needed to close.

"Amazing what happens when you're not wearing a rock on your finger," he commented to me. I looked up from the money I was counting.

"What do you mean?" I asked.

"Oh c'mon, you didn't notice? Those guys were all waiting around for you," he said. I hadn't realized it until he said it. "Maybe I should walk you home," he offered.

"It's okay. I can take care of myself," I said.

"I'd feel better about it if I walked you home. You're on the way to my apartment anyway," he said. I agreed, and we made our way to my place. We didn't say much, but the weather was so nice it ended up being a pleasant walk.

"This is me," I said as we reached my apartment. He looked up at the apartment and then back down at me.

"Cool, I'll see you tomorrow," he said, turning to walk away.

"Do you want to come in?" I offered. "Maybe have a drink?"

He was hesitant at first but then accepted the offer.

When we got into the apartment, he stood in the living room, looking around. "I don't have Jameson; you want Jack and coke?" I yelled from the kitchen.

"Sure," he said, sitting down on the couch. I came in and handed him his drink as I took a sip of my vodka soda.

"I got all new furniture; new mattress too," I said proudly.

"See, I told you that bank account would come in handy," he said, looking around at the furniture, his hand grazing the couch cushions.

"There's something I want to talk to you about, being you're a professional player and all," I said. He put his drink down on the coffee table and folded his hands on his lap, leaning in closer to me.

"Professional player?"

"You know what I mean," I said. He rolled his eyes.

"If I were professional, I would get paid for it. I don't, though. But, go ahead – continue. What do you need my 'expert' advice with?" He asked.

"How do I have sex?" He let out a chuckle until he realized I was serious.

"Wait, you're being serious? Really? That's what you need help with? I mean, judging from last week, it seems to me you know how to do it pretty well," he said. I could feel my cheeks getting warm with embarrassment.

"No, I mean, how do I get a guy to want to have casual sex with me without coming off like a slut?" I elaborated.

"What do you mean? You flirt all the time at work; you know how to play the game," he answered.

"Yeah, I know how to play the game when it isn't real. But, like, how do I close the deal?" He stayed silent for a minute like he didn't know how to answer the question.

"Um, okay. Let's pretend we're at a bar, and I come over to you like that guy did that night we went out... Is this seat taken?" He asked, now changing his voice like he was role-playing.

"It is now," I replied as if I were indicating he should sit.

We went back and forth with role-playing as if we were strangers flirting at a bar.

"I like that shirt on you. It brings out your eyes," he said.

"Thanks. How about you come back home with me and see what my eyes look like with it off," I answered. He squinted his eyes, nearly choking on his drink.

"Okay, that was a bit aggressive," he said.

"See! I have no idea what I'm doing!" I sighed. "I've never had casual sex before; I've always been in relationships."

He put his drink on the coffee table, putting his hand on my thigh, he came in closer. "Trust me. You are going to be fine. You'll know what to say when the time is right – and how to say it. It really isn't that hard."

I placed my hand on top of his. For some strange reason, being with him made me feel better about – well, everything. He was the only consistent thing in my life at the time. Being with him that night, I somehow felt safe with him, even if it was just sex. Struggling for the right words, I finally said: "Will you stay with me tonight? I don't want to be alone."

"See! That's better! You aren't going straight to sex. You're just saying, 'stay with me', which means he'll still have to work a little. That's actually perfect, well done!" I didn't move, just stared directly at him. He looked down at my hand on his, then turned his head and looked at me. "Wait, are we still role-playing, or are you asking me to stay with you?"

"I'm asking you to stay with me," I replied. I knew it was a risky move; Mia was right. He was my boss. But at that moment, I felt like I needed to be with him again. Staring at him sitting on my couch, I suddenly craved his touch.

He took his hand off my thigh and picked his drink back up. He took a sip and cleared his throat.

"I'm sorry, I didn't mean to make you feel uncomfortable. You don't have to...." He cut me off.

"I never said I was uncomfortable – or that I wouldn't," he said. "You just took me off guard."

He took another sip of his drink, put it back on the coffee table, and slid himself closer to me. He placed his hand back on my thigh and leaned in to kiss me. As I leaned into his kiss, I lifted his shirt off and started unbuttoning his pants. Sliding his pants off, I slowly made my way down his chest with my tongue. When I got to his stomach, I had almost forgotten how solid and toned it was, and at that moment, all I wanted to do was pleasure him. He laid back as I started going down on him until he got to the point that he was about to orgasm, but he pulled me back up. I took his hands in mine and led him up and into my bedroom. "Let's go break in that new mattress," he said, following me. When we were done, we both stayed immobile, looking up at the ceiling.

"Well, I'm trying to justify how to put this in a 'one-time' category and just can't seem to come up with anything," he said, turning his head to look at me.

"Booty call?" I suggested.

"We don't 'call' each other," he shot down.

"Friends with benefits?" He came up with.

"We're not exactly friends," I argued.

He thought for a minute. "Why do we need a label? We're just us, having secret sex," he said.

"I like that – secret sex," I repeated. He rolled his body over, now wholly facing me.

"You're my sexy little secret," he said, smiling.

"It's actually perfect. I'm not looking for anything, and you're incapable of falling in love. You're the ideal candidate. Everyone who starts out saying it's casual sex ends up falling in love. It's in every rom-com. That could never happen with us. You can be like my..." I thought for a second. "My significant nobody."

With his eyebrows raised and smile widened, he said, "I like that." With that, James became my 'significant nobody'.

Every Friday and Saturday night for the next few months, we went home together, once we decided my place or his. We became comfortable with each other sexually almost immediately. After only the first couple of times, we learned precisely how to turn each other on. I still hadn't viewed him as a freak of any kind, but he was undeniably the best sex I ever had. He was passionate and sensual, and incredibly attentive. He got me out of my comfort zone, trying positions I had never done before. For the first time in my life, he made me feel sexy. Our little secret hadn't affected our working relationship, and neither of us was jealous when the other flirted with someone else.

It was already sometime in April when he texted me one Friday night that he would be late. He said he had an issue to deal with, when a good-looking Black boy walked into a bar with a very pretty young girl. Neither one looked like they could be older than seventeen. They sat at the bar as I approached them. "Do you have an ID?" I asked.

"We're not ordering liquor," he said.

"You can't sit here," I said and turned around to head to the other side of the bar to help another customer. The boy followed me to the other side and patiently waited for me to fill the order.

"Excuse me, Miss," he said politely. "Is James here?"

"No, not yet. He's tied up with something. He'll be in later," I answered.

"I'm his nephew, Christopher," he said. I looked down at him skeptically. "I am," he insisted.

"I know his brother, and he doesn't have children. Nice try, though," I answered.

"No, not that brother. His other brother," he said.

"Oh yeah? What's his name?" I questioned.

"James," he responded. I rolled my eyes.

"So, both brothers have the same name, James?" I asked.

"Yes," he began. "Text him and ask."

"I'm not bothering him with this," I simply answered. He picked up his phone as if he were going to text him. I leaned my elbow on the bar and watched him, silently daring him to text him. He put his phone away.

"What's your name?" He asked me.

"Amber."

He leaned in over the bar. "Amber, look, I don't want to bother him if he's busy. You see that girl I'm with? It's our first date, and I am trying to impress her. Please don't give me a hard time in front of her," he pleaded. I looked over at the girl and back at him. He had an adorable dimple that appeared when he smiled.

"You're trying to impress a girl? You're quite clearly not related to James," I said as I scoured the bar looking at the tables. "Go sit at the table in the back, in the corner. You better not repeat I allowed this, and no ordering alcohol!" I said sternly. I couldn't help it; he seemed sincere, and I was a sucker. He thanked me and made his way to the corner table.

James finally arrived around eight, visibly aggravated. "Everything okay?" I asked.

He took an order from a customer, and while starting

to make the drink, he said: "A pipe broke in my bathroom, and there was water all over the damn place. The plumber is coming tomorrow morning. It took me two hours just to get the water out. Luckily nothing seems too damaged." I didn't say anything; I could tell he was in a bad mood. A few minutes later, he looked around the bar, and while focused on the boy in the corner, asked me: "Who's serving table two?" I froze and looked down.

"I am," I muttered under my breath. He was now looking over to get a better look at the table.

"Is he with a girl?" He asked.

"Yes," I replied.

A huge smile grew across his face. "He took my advice! Okay, listen, here's what you're going to do, when you bring him the bill, whatever bill he hands you, just break it down into change and don't charge him. But make it look like he paid the bill – get it?"

I looked up, speechless. "Are you coaching teenagers now?" I finally managed to say.

He laughed. "He's my nephew," he replied. I did as he instructed and watched the boy wink at James as he left.

At the end of the night, after Kaitlyn left, James and I were closing up. Completely forgetting what had happened earlier, I announced there was a discrepancy. "How much?" He asked.

"$42.38," I said.

"Oh, that must be Christopher's bill," he said, reaching into his pocket and handing me the money to include in the register. I took the money from his hand, embarrassed.

"I feel so bad. I didn't believe that he was your nephew. I gave him a real hard time," I said.

"What? Why wouldn't you believe he's my nephew?

We look exactly alike," he answered, so seriously. I looked up at him in silence, not sure how to respond. He finally smiled. "It's a joke; we obviously look nothing alike."

I let out a sigh. "I thought you were losing it for a minute," I laughed.

"He didn't mention you were busting his balls. As a matter of fact, he said nice things about you," he answered.

"What did he say?" I asked, now very curious.

He pulled out his phone and started reading his texts. "He said: 'Thanks again, you da man, worked like a charm'. Winky face. Then new text, 'even got a kiss'. Then another new text, 'by the way Amber is crazy hot, hope you're hitting that'."

"He did not say that!" I said, reaching for his phone. He held it high above his head, backing up against the counter.

"He did!" He argued, laughing.

"Show me," I said, now between his legs reaching up for his phone. He put his left hand on my waist and slightly pushed me back in front of him as his eyes slowly scanned me up and down, undressing me.

"I love to play show and tell," he said flirtatiously. "Tease me. Show me what color bra you're wearing, and I'll show you the text."

I bit my bottom lip and slowly started lifting my shirt. He watched in a trance as I lifted it above my chest and exposed the black lace bra I was wearing. He pulled me back into him, kissing me. "That's hot, my place or yours?" He asked as I grabbed his phone. I looked down at the texts Christopher had sent him. The first two parts were true, but the next two texts read differently than he described.

"Amber is really nice. You should try impressing her."

"And don't worry, she totally ID'd me."

I handed him back the phone. "You have the plumber coming, right? We can go to yours."

Chapter Six

It was pouring the next night, with people making their way to the bar: some holding umbrellas, some soaked from the rain. I didn't even recognize Evan with his baseball cap on until I went over to serve him and came into direct eye contact with him. I stood frozen for a second. The red in his eyes and the expression on his face immediately gave away how drunk he was.

"I need to talk to you," he slurred.

"Evan, look around – it's really busy in here. I don't have time for this tonight," I said, starting to turn to the next customer.

"I want a drink," he said.

I probably shouldn't have served him, considering the level of intoxication he appeared to be in, but I gave him a drink to appease him. He was quiet for about five minutes before he yelled over the bar for another. James' head turned as he looked him up and down, then to me.

"Is that who I think it is?" He asked. I simply nodded. He approached Evan.

"What can I get you?" He asked.

"Amber," he replied.

"Unless you're referring to a specific type of ale, the answer is no," James said sternly.

"Make me a drink, bar boy," Evan said.

"I'm going to deny that request as well. You look like you've had enough already," James answered.

"Who the fuck are you to tell me when I've had enough?" Evan said, getting louder.

James started cracking the knuckles on his hand with his thumb. He leaned over the bar to Evan. "I'm going to ask you nicely to leave."

Evan leaned forward on his stool, his elbows resting on the bar, mimicking James' stance. Now, looking him dead in the eye, he said daringly, "Make me."

My attention went to the bouncer, Tony, as I signaled for him to intervene. Dressed in all black, Tony stood about six foot six, arms covered in tattoos and biceps that appeared as if his gym of choice was the yard of prisons. He was the type of intimidating guy you would cross the street to avoid in the dark. He handed an ID back to a person at the door as he turned around to make his way over. James looked up and put his hand up in the air, in a silent gesture not to come closer.

"I don't need a bouncer for you," James snarled, staring directly at Evan. Kaitlyn and I stood still as we watched the face-off between Evan and James.

"You think I'm stupid?" Evan began. "I know all about

you and Amber. I have big eyes!"

"That big eye of yours is going to be a big black eye if you don't leave," James warned.

"Is this what you do for fun? You go around fucking people's girls, or was it just mine you wanted?" Evan asked.

"I don't know what you're talking about, man," James said. "But I am not going to ask you again to leave. Not nicely, at least."

"I know you have been fucking Amber this whole time; I'm not an asshole. I always knew there was something between the two of you. You guys couldn't be any more obvious. Now, I'm coming to take back what's mine."

Evan wasn't typically a drinker; I had never seen him so drunk. Not to mention so bold, going up on James like that who was probably twice his size. James smirked and waved his hand in the air, turning his back to him to walk away. Evan grabbed a beer bottle from the bar and chucked it. I was shocked to see the reflexes on James to dodge a bottle from behind so effortlessly. Suddenly, he flew around to the other side of the bar, grabbed Evan by the neck, and dragged him physically out of the bar. Tony started covering the door with his body to prevent a scene while Kaitlyn and I followed behind.

"James, he's drunk. Leave him alone," I pleaded. James shoved Evan to the wet concrete and turned around to come back in. Evan stumbling to get up and regain his posture, lunged at him and sucker-punched him from behind. Covering his face as he fell headfirst into the brick wall, James now turned around to approach Evan again.

"You want to fight?" James asked, getting rowdier.

I desperately looked over at Tony, who put his hand on James' shoulder.

"Don't waste your time with this asshole," he said calmly.

James walked right over to Evan, standing at least four inches higher than him, looking down at him.

"I'm going to let you off easy this time, but this is your warning. This is a place of business. If you come in here again like you did, no one is going to stop me from giving you the beating you deserve," he said and walked back into the bar. I looked over at Evan.

"If I wasn't clear the first time, let me elaborate. I never want to see you again," I said before going back into the bar.

Later that night, sitting in James' living room, I changed into a dry t-shirt he had given me.

"I'm really sorry about Evan," I said. He went into the entertainment room and returned with a bottle of Jameson and two shot glasses. He poured us both a shot.

"I have a feeling this is going to be a long 'Evan' night," he said, rattling his glass into mine and taking a shot.

"I just can't believe after all this time he showed up," I said as I took my shot.

"Actually, I am surprised it took him this long. Did you honestly expect him to just leave your life without even trying to get you back?" He asked.

"Well yeah, I mean, he cheated on me. How in love with me could he have been?" I reasoned.

"Just because he cheated on you doesn't mean he didn't love you. People cheat all the time for different reasons."

"Oh yeah? Like what?" I asked.

"Anything. Maybe he saw a quick opportunity to get his nuts off and didn't think you'd find out. It could have had nothing to do with you at all," he explained.

"Get his nuts off? C'mon, it's not like we didn't have sex," I said.

"You're missing the point. Men, even women, don't necessarily cheat because of lack of sex. You said she wasn't even pretty," he reminded me.

"Yes, but I also said I might have been exaggerating."

"I'm sure she wasn't as pretty as you. Not many girls are," he said. I sat taken back by his statement.

"You think I am that pretty?" I asked, stunned. Evan never really complimented me or told me I was pretty. It was nice to hear a man say that; I often questioned if I really was.

"So, that thing he said, about the big eyes. What do you think he meant by that?" He asked, avoiding my question.

"Who knows, he was drunk," I answered, hoping James didn't catch on to what Evan was alluding to.

"I know, but he said he knew there was something between us for years. You think he thought you liked me or that I liked you?" I shifted my eyes from his. I knew exactly what Evan meant; he had been telling me for years that I was in love with James. Always implying that I was either sleeping with him or wanted to.

I put the glass on the coffee table and put my arms around his neck. Then, sliding myself onto his lap, I started kissing his neck. "I think you're putting too much thought into it. I think he's crazy. Who cares what he thinks?"

He ran his hand through my hair and pulled my head back to look at him. "You're right. Who cares," he said, pulling my lips into his. Without hesitation, he picked me up and carried me into the entertainment room.

Chapter Seven

The only thing worse than being sick is being sick in the middle of the summer. I woke up so congested, I tried to muster through it but nothing was working. After a steaming hot shower, I could barely hold my head up. The thought of standing behind a bar for twelve hours made me dizzy. I texted Kaitlyn and asked her to cover for me and slept most of the day. At around one a.m. I got a text from James: *Sick or with a dude?* It made me laugh. As a matter of fact, it was the first time I had smiled all day. *Concerned or jealous?* I replied. It took a few minutes for him to answer, and then I got one word: *Curious.*

When I told him I really was sick, he asked if I had taken anything. I told him I had no energy to go to the store, and he said the bar was hectic at the moment, but he could run out in an hour and get me some things. When

I opened the door, he took a step back as if he were afraid to get any closer. "Wow, you look *really* sick," he commented, walking in with a bag. "Do you have a fever?"

"I don't know, I didn't take my temperature. I've been in bed all day," I answered. He followed me into the bedroom and sat on the side of the bed when I laid back down. He reached into the bag and started placing over-the-counter medicines he had purchased on my night table. He took out a container of soup he had got from the Chinese restaurant down the block. "Aw, are you taking care of me?" I joked.

"I just need you back at work," he said simply. Then he felt my head. "You definitely have a fever." I reached over and took some of the medicine off the night table.

"You better go now before I get you sick also," I warned. "Thank you for bringing this stuff." He got up to walk out of the room.

"No problem – do you want to give me your key? I'll come back after closing to make sure you're okay."

"I don't want to get you sick," I replied.

"It's okay. I'll sleep on the couch," he offered. I told him where the key was, and James did exactly what he said he would. He came back after closing and slept on the couch. He did that for three nights straight.

The next Friday night, we ended up at his place after closing. Although we had become extremely comfortable with each other sexually, we were never really intimate. We didn't speak much about anything other than sex, and we didn't cuddle. It was more of a silent business deal than a relationship. The only thing we did in bed after was sleep. We always spent the night, though, and then one of us did the walk of shame the next day. As I was getting up out of his bed that next morning and putting on my clothes, I couldn't help but stare at his bare chest as he stayed in bed. I walked over closer, examining the tattoo around his neck. "Did that hurt?" I asked.

"Not really. When they got to the back of the neck, maybe a little," he answered. I sat back down on the bed next to him.

"I really want one," I said.

He smiled while his eyes undressed my body. "What were you thinking?"

I touched the side of my hip. "Something here, maybe flames," I said.

"That sounds hot," he said.

"What do the numbers mean?" I asked, now running my finger gently along the inked dog tag.

"My friend James, it was his birthday," he answered.

"Christopher's dad?" I asked, remembering the good-looking Black boy who had come into the bar months earlier that referred to James as his uncle.

"Yeah, he was my best friend when we were in the army. We called him Jim, to differentiate between the two of us."

"You were in the army?" I asked, shocked. It explained his beer bottle reflexes; he had professional training.

"Yeah, I fought in the war; did four years in Afghanistan. He was like my brother. So different than my real brother; mature, respected, and a hell of a soldier. I admired him so much; I would have loved to be like him. He didn't make it back, so I make sure I'm active in Christopher's life."

I didn't know what to say. In a million years, I wouldn't have taken James for a soldier.

"That must have been really bad," I said, moving closer to him.

"You ever hear of a war that's good?" He asked.

"I'm sorry, I had no idea."

"I don't like talking about it," he said. I placed my hand down on his chest. He put his hand over mine and lifted it off him. "Don't look at me like that."

"Like what?" I asked, taken back. He got off the bed and picked his t-shirt up off the floor, pulling it over his head.

"Like I'm some sort of victim, like there's something wrong with me," he began. "All you girls think the same thing... 'oh explains why he's damaged', 'I can change him', 'must be why he's a dick'. Well, I got news for you – I was a dick before, and I'm a dick now. Has nothing to do with anything!" He was getting angrier as he kept going, while simultaneously looking for his pants, flinging loose clothing out of his way. I had never seen this side of him. I didn't know what to do; he was clearly upset.

"I should go," I said, turning to leave.

"Fine, see ya," he replied.

I had made it all the way to the corner when I stood still. I don't know why I left. I guess I just panicked. He was noticeably bothered, and I had no idea how to help him. This guy I thought I knew so well had so much more to him than I could have ever known. He fought in a war; he took care of me when I was sick and cared for his friend's son as if he were his own nephew. A far cry from the selfish, arrogant asshole I always assumed he was. I was the bitch in this scenario.

Slowly, I turned back around and made my way to his door. When he opened the door, I did the first thing that came to mind. Standing on my tippy toes, I kissed him. Without taking his lips off me, he aggressively dragged me back inside and sat on the couch, pulling me on top of him. Neither of us said a word, stripping each other's clothes off. In the heat of the moment, it just happened. He was in me, passionately moving me up and down on him as my tongue explored his neck. He squeezed my hips harder, pulling me into him until he said he was close and lifted me up. When he finished, he released his grip, and I slumped back down on his lap. I attempted to get up when he pulled me back down on him, his arms around me, my head on his shoulder.

"Don't move, don't get up," he whispered, between breaths.

"We're in a mess," I said.

He started running his hand up and down my spine. "It's okay. Just stay here a second."

Our hearts were beating so intensely that in that second, it seemed in sync.

"So that's why guys hate condoms!" He said, laughing.

"You never had sex without a condom before?" I asked, amazed.

"No, I never trusted anyone enough," he answered.

"You trust me that much?"

"Yeah, I trust you with everything. You run my business with me. I can tell you anything. You're like my best friend, only we have amazing sex," he said, now pushing my hair out of my face and staring into my eyes. "And you're a really good kisser," he added, slipping his tongue in my mouth again.

"Pete doesn't kiss you like this?" I asked playfully, referring to his best friend.

"No, not yet at least," he joked. "You know what else? You're fucking awesome," he continued.

I laughed. "Oh, I know how awesome I am," I replied. I was glad I went back after all.

Chapter Eight

It was the Wednesday night before I was leaving for my birthday trip to New Orleans, my once upon a time bachelorette party. I was lost in the fantasy of what the next week would have in store for me as I counted out the register when I heard the bell to the door chime. Without looking up, I said, "We're closed."

As I listened to the footsteps drawing nearer, I glanced in the mirror in front of me to see James walking up to a bar stool and sitting down. I turned around to the bar, rested my elbows on it, and leaned towards him. "Can I help you?" I asked.

He smiled. "I'll just take a spicy redhead to go, please," he answered. It was the first time we had been sleeping together in the five months that he showed interest in being with me other than a Friday or Saturday night after work. I wouldn't be returning until Monday, so I took him up on the offer and went to his place.

The second we got through the door, we were all over each other. Peeling off each other's clothes as he pushed me towards the room. Kissing my neck, he whispered in my ear: "I need to make sure you're satisfied before going crazy in Nola." I ran my fingers through his hair, pulling him into me.

"Would you be jealous?" I whispered back in a taunting voice.

His lips began traveling down my body as he simply answered: "No." I lifted his head from my stomach and pulled my body back a little.

"Not at all?" I asked, trying to sound sad.

He licked his lips and smiled. "Why would I be jealous? No one can do it like me," he said with confidence as he reached into his night table drawer for a condom. He was searching through the drawer with his hand until he pushed himself up and looked in. Annoyed, he got up and went over to his jeans on the floor. He took the condom out of his wallet. As he ripped it open, he remarked, "The last one, got to make this count." He lived up to his promise. After, as he lay in bed, I started getting up to find my clothes.

"Hate to hit and run out, but my flight is at seven a.m. I need to make sure I have everything packed."

"When do you get back again?" He asked. He knew the answer. I must have told him five times.

"Monday night," I replied. He nodded in acknowledgment, and I headed home.

We all met at Mia's the next day to go to the airport together. Originally there were seven of us going for my bachelorette party, but because three of the girls in my bridal party were Evan's sisters, it was only four of us. Me and Mia, and our two close friends Erica and Payton. Mia and I didn't get to see them too often; they didn't run in our nighttime crew. Erica worked in a beauty shop, and she always got the best make-up and accessories for all of us. She was Spanish and was always well made up. She stood about five foot seven and had a huge chest that was so perfect that even though they were natural, they appeared fake. She had gorgeous green eyes that matched her olive complexion and long dark, curly hair that seemed to always be in a different style every time we saw her.

Payton was shorter than me, standing about five foot one, looking incredibly young for her age. At almost thirty, she looked more like she was seventeen and was asked for ID no matter where we went. She wore thick glasses over her bright blue eyes and dressed very modestly. It didn't help that she always wore her brunette hair in a ponytail. She was a pharmacist and probably the smartest person I knew. She didn't wear any make-up at all and was very serious most of the time.

The flight was under four hours. By the time we arrived at the hotel, we were already a little tipsy from drinking on the plane. As we wheeled our luggage into the lobby with difficulty from the broken-up concrete outside, I realized I probably should have packed more flats than the four pairs of heels I took. As if she were reading my mind, Erica said:

"Should we place bets on who is going to be the first to bust their ass?"

We laughed as we headed up to the check-in counter. We had gotten two rooms. Mia and I would be sharing one, and Erica and Payton would share the other. We agreed on meeting back in the lobby in an hour to give us time to unpack and get ready to find a place for lunch.

"This room is so tiny!" Mia frowned as she walked in. I looked around. The space was incredibly small considering it held two full-size beds, but there wasn't much more than that—a dresser that held a TV on top of it and a small desk in the corner. I opened my suitcase and took out the clothes, putting them in the dresser drawers as Mia sat on her bed.

"You aren't going to unpack?" I asked, eying her suitcase on the floor.

"Nah, not yet," she answered, looking at her phone. "God, I hate Rob. The man lives in Miami and yet still finds the time to aggravate me on a daily basis!"

"What's his problem now?" I asked.

"Oh, now he's saying he didn't know I was taking off this weekend. I only told him like twelve times. He is such an airhead! Is James like that?" She asked.

"Not really," I said, trying not to look at her. She stood up and came closer to me, and smirked.

"Okay, let me rephrase the question. Was James like that *before* he was your secret boyfriend?"

I shook my head and looked at her. "He's not my boyfriend. We have casual sex, that is it," I said.

"Oh right, that is it," she began. "So then, you are going to hook up if given the opportunity while here?"

I started ruffling through the clothes I had just placed in the drawer.

"Did he stick his finger in your ass yet?" She asked. I felt my cheeks flush. She stomped her feet on the ground as she laughed hysterically. "Ah, I knew it! I love it. I love

77

it. I love it!" She exclaimed dramatically.

"Are you wearing that, or are you changing?" I asked, still digging through the contents.

"My question first," she said, getting serious now. I shut the drawer and looked at her.

"He called me his 'best friend' last night," I said.

"And had he said, 'secret girlfriend' instead of 'best friend' that would change your intentions?" She asked.

"I have no idea what I am going to do while I am here, but I can assure you whether I do or don't hook up with someone has nothing at all to do with James."

"Oh, I wonder if he is going to take you to Rob's wedding!" She asked, clapping her hands in excitement. "You have no idea how much money they are throwing down on this wedding; it's going to be insane!" His brother was getting married in Miami in November, which nobody, including James, could understand. When it came to players, Rob topped that list.

"We're not a couple, Mia. Did you hear what I said? He said I was his best friend. You don't go to a wedding in Miami with your best friend."

She let out a laugh. "I see," she said. "Yes, I am changing. Just putting on a romper and sneakers, we will probably be walking around a lot. I will change again before we go out tonight. You?"

I looked down. I was already wearing distressed shorts and a tank top. "I'll stay like this if we are changing again. Also, do not mention James in front of the other girls. You know that, right?"

She rolled her eyes. "Yes, I know that. I did say your *secret* boyfriend, didn't I?" I didn't answer her. I waited until she changed, and we headed down to meet Erica and Payton.

Walking down Bourbon Street was complete mayhem. I didn't think anywhere could be more crowded than New York City, but boy was I wrong. This was so different. People were drinking in the streets during broad daylight, all wearing beads around their necks. I worked in a bar and didn't experience the level of drunk people I saw just walking to find a restaurant. All the bars and buildings seemed to have balconies, and an overflow of people hanging off them. There were bodies everywhere you looked; right, left, up, down. Literally *down*, people were lying on the streets.

Mia and Erica smiled at each other like naughty schoolgirls knowing they would get themselves into trouble. Payton was utterly unimpressed by the entire scene, and I was nervous. I don't know why I was scared; I was just completely out of my comfort zone. I went from having a serious relationship for five years to having a "secret boyfriend" or whatever he was for the past five months. Being single and accessible in a place like New Orleans was not something I was used to.

When we settled on a place to eat, Payton immediately ordered a shot. I looked at her, surprised. "What? I need to get out of my head to be in this filthy place. It's so humid I already feel like I need another shower," she explained. We sat in the restaurant for two hours, eating, drinking, and discussing the game plan for the week. My birthday was Friday night, so we needed to figure out what to do before and after.

After getting the bill, we decided we would do our own pub crawl down the French Quarter, check out all the bars and the stores along the way. We planned to have one drink in every bar and then move on. That was our plan. I don't think that any of us expected that one drink would be a shot for Payton. By the third stop, she was inebriated.

As she stumbled out of the bar, with the three of us trailing behind her, she approached a group of guys who seemed about our age, and all decked out in beads. "Did you have to show your tits for those?" she asked.

"We did. You want one; what are you going to show?" One of the guys answered her.

"What would you like to see?" She slurred. Erica took her by the arm and pulled her back.

"Okay, Pay, let's go," she said

"I want beads," Payton whined.

Suddenly, without warning, she lifted her shirt and exposed her bare chest to the group. They started clapping, which excited her more. She was now trying to raise the shirt over her head and take it off. As Erica tried to pull her back, Mia and I surrounded her trying to block their view of her.

"Stop being prudes; you're in Nola!" One of the guys said. He came between Mia and me and, looking at Payton, urged her on. "Take it off, sweetheart."

Erica was now physically trying to keep Payton from taking her shirt off, and Payton became violently angered.

"Leave me alone, Erica! Why can't I be a slut today? I'm on vacation. You're a slut every day; what's your excuse?"

"Excuse me?" Erica snarled, looking Payton up and down. Seeing that there was about to be a fight excited the guys. They started cheering and egging them on. "You're a sloppy drunk," Erica said, turning her back on her when Payton shoved her.

Without hesitation, Erica swirled around and pushed

her back with such force Payton fell to the ground. I ran to help Payton get up, and Mia grabbed Erica's back, trying to calm her down. Trying to help Payton up was like trying to lift a dead body. She wasn't helping at all. Finally, just as she was almost balanced, she lost her grip and fell back down. Trying to push herself up, she started vomiting all over the floor, all over my sneakers.

Disgusted, the guys left up the block, and all three of us had to drag Payton's body down Bourbon Street back to the hotel with much difficulty. Day one, not even seven p.m., and we were already doing the walk of shame.

Chapter Nine

The next morning, we went to a breakfast place a few blocks from the hotel, which was known for its Bloody Mary's. Payton stared at hers in disgust as the three of us inhaled ours.

"You guys make up, or do we need to get a bouncer for the night?" Mia asked. Payton looked down, ashamed of herself.

"Yes, we made up. Stop looking so embarrassed, Pay. A lot of people get obnoxious when they drink too much," Erica laughed, pushing Payton's drink towards her.

"Drink it. It will make you feel better," I said. She just shook her head. "It's my birthday; you need to do whatever I want!" I demanded.

She looked up at me, gave me a half-smile, and took a sip of the drink. She tried to apologize, but we all brushed it off. We were in New Orleans; we were not about to let one stupid night ruin our moods. Especially on my thirtieth birthday. That day went much better. We made a 'no shot' rule and took the drinking a little slower, so we had the energy to go out at night.

As we were shopping, I passed by a lingerie store and saw a ridiculously hot outfit on the mannequin. As if it were calling my name, I walked right into the store. Following me in, the girls descended to different racks. I went right over to the piece I'd seen in the window. An older lady who worked there came over to help me. She had gray hair and glasses, a bit thick, and dressed in a pair of jeans and an oversized cardigan. She looked more like a librarian than a salesperson in a lingerie shop.

"That comes in red or black. Which would you prefer?" she asked. My eyes shifted away from her in embarrassment. This particular piece of lingerie was raunchier than anything I owned. I had sexy nightgowns and teddys, don't get me wrong, but this was an outfit that would be better suited for dancing on a pole. It was so skimpy and sheer; the lace was practically see-through. A memory of James on top of me flickered through my mind. Him holding me by my hair, aggressively pulling me into him, softly biting my shoulder. "I love you in red," he had whispered. I could feel myself blushing again as I suddenly had a bit of excitement trickle down my body.

"Red," I replied. She smiled.

"Yes, red would be lovely. It matches your hair beautifully," she said as she turned around to retrieve my outfit. Lovely? Beautiful? Not synonyms I would use to describe the ensemble. As I went to the register to pay for it, the girls gathered around. I looked at all three of them who hadn't had anything in their hands to purchase.

"Am I the only one buying something?" I asked, uncomfortable.

"Someone is planning on having fun tonight," Erica giggled. I shot a look at Mia, who knew exactly why I was buying it. She inched closer to me and leaned into my ear.

"You're my best friend, and never once have I considered buying you lingerie while on vacation." I rolled my eyes.

"Let's see what the night holds," I laughed, paying for it and taking the bag from the cashier.

After shopping, we had a few drinks and then changed for our night out. We were going for a nice dinner, then going out barhopping.

When we got to the restaurant, the place was packed. The tables were so close to each other that you could hear everyone's conversations. Unlike a lot of the other places we passed, this restaurant was pretty classy. White linen tablecloths, not paper. A glass case under the bar displayed raw clams, oysters, shrimp, and lobsters all laid out on ice. The smell of seafood mixed with Cajun spices and grilled steaks lingered through the air.

After we were seated, I looked up from the menu. "You guys want to share an order of barbeque oysters?" I asked.

Before anyone could answer, a very good-looking guy at the table next to us leaned over and said: "You should try the charbroiled ones."

I turned my head to face him; there was barely any room between our tables. He had dirty blond hair, brown eyes, and a very neatly shaped beard. He was well built, with a piece of a black and red tattoo peeping out from under his black t-shirt. He was with two other guys, all just as good-looking.

"Is that right?" I asked, batting my eyes. He leaned in a bit closer.

"I mean, the barbeque ones are good also, but the charbroiled are amazing," he elaborated.

"Let's do both," Mia said, smiling at his friend.

"Where are you girls from?" His friend asked.

"New York," Mia responded. "And you guys?"

"Florida," he answered.

Before long, both tables were pushed together, and we were all eating, drinking, and laughing together. Anyone in that restaurant would have easily assumed we had all known each other for years. Trevor, sitting right next to me, was very interested in it being my birthday. He thought I looked a lot younger than thirty. His friends, Danny and Kyle, were engaging the girls with conversation. Danny was the youngest of the three, only twenty-five, with blond hair, blue eyes, and was clean-shaven. Kyle's style was similar to Trevor's. He had tattoos down both his arms, a beard, dark hair, and dark brown eyes. They were both thirty-two. I was playing a game in my head the entire time, trying to decide which one of them was the cutest.

When the bill came, the guys insisted on picking it up and splitting it between the three of them. "Where are we going now?" Danny asked. The four of us all looked at each other silently, knowing we were all thinking the same thing. Of course, there were only three of them and four of us.

"We just got in yesterday. We haven't really got to explore the scene yet. Where do you suggest?" Erica asked. They suggested a bar they had passed the night before, and soon we were at a very crowded bar nearby: two floors, a bar on each, and a stage where people were singing karaoke.

"Birthday shots!" Trevor said, handing us all shots that he took upon himself to order.

"We said no shots," Payton said, nudging me.

"We said no shots during the *day*, it's nighttime now," I reasoned, as we took the shots.

We hung out for two hours, dancing, taking shots, Kyle going back and forth between Erica and Mia, and Payton with Danny. Trevor was by my side the entire night, drinking and dancing with me, while holding a good conversation. I was having such a good time with him; I hadn't thought about James much at all. Finally, I started digging through my pocketbook for my cigarettes. "I'm going out for a smoke," I bellowed over the music. He nodded in acknowledgment and followed me out.

When we got outside, I lit my cigarette and leaned against the wall.

"You know, smoking stunts your growth," Trevor said, slowly eying me up and down. Easy for him to say, he was at least six foot three.

I smiled sarcastically. "Ah, and there explains the motive behind the five-inch heel," I said, motioning towards my shoes. "It was intended for all of us short smokers out there."

He let out a laugh. "You're funny," he remarked.

"Am I?" I asked playfully.

He came in closer to me. "You are. You're hot too," he continued.

"Yeah, *smoking*," I laughed, blowing smoke in his face.

"If I'm going to inhale secondhand smoke, I would

rather get it this way," he said, leaning down to kiss me. I dropped my cigarette to the floor, and I started running my hands up his biceps. He pulled me in closer to him, running his hands down my back, grabbing me from behind. I pulled him in closer, clenching the back of his neck. Backing up from me, he took me by the hand and led me behind the alleyway where it wasn't so crowded.

Now he was against the wall pulling me into him; I could feel him getting aroused under his jeans. As we kissed, he ran his hands down my chest, around my waist, and then back around until he was rubbing me between the legs. I was getting more turned on by the minute when unexpectedly, the image of James ran through my mind. His hands on me, his tongue in my mouth, him feeling the need to 'satisfy' me before I left. I felt like I could smell him, feel him, picture him saying he wouldn't be jealous if I were to be with someone else. I could hear his voice as if he were whispering in my brain: *No one can do it like me.*

I pulled back from Trevor's embrace. "What's wrong?" He asked. The truth was I had no idea what was wrong. James wasn't my boyfriend; he was probably with another girl at that exact moment. But for some reason, I couldn't get him out of my head – like he was haunting me. It was almost as if I felt *guilty*. Trevor was hot and turned me on, but he wasn't James.

"I don't feel good," I lied.

"Are you going to be sick?" He asked.

"Maybe, I think I just need to lay down. I am going to go back to my hotel room," I said.

"You sure? Maybe you just need to eat something," he offered.

"No, I'm sure. Will you tell the girls I went back to the room?" I asked.

He said okay and took my phone number. As I headed back to the hotel, my phone vibrated. *Mia* flashed across the screen. I told her I would see her later on and to stay out and not worry, that I didn't feel good, and now they were better suited, three and three.

So to be clear... Trevor is fair game? She texted.

Yeah, go for it, I typed back.

You sure you're okay? Do you want me to come back to the room? She asked.

I'm fine, just have a headache. Going to bed, have fun xoxo

I walked into the hotel room and sat on my bed. What the hell was I doing? I had no idea how I was feeling or why I was even thinking about James. My phone vibrated again. This time it was Trevor asking if I made it back to the hotel okay. I answered *yes.* I started taking off my dress and changing into my pajamas when the phone vibrated again. *Erica.* Now she was asking me if I was coming back. Were they kidding me? My God, why couldn't I just go back to my room if I wanted? Why was everyone so concerned with where or how I was?

Annoyed, I threw the phone back on the bed and brushed my teeth. As I walked out of the bathroom, it vibrated again. Now I was completely irritated. I picked up the phone, ready to go off on whoever it was, when *Biggest Asshole* came across the screen. Stunned, I slowly sat down on the bed and opened his text: *Happy Birthday Sexy*

I smiled to myself and looked at the time. It was midnight, which meant it was one a.m. in New York – he must still be at work and waited until the last minute of my birthday to text me. I waited half an hour then simply responded, *thanks.*

Chapter Ten

I ate breakfast by myself at a café nearby, waiting for the girls to wake up. Mia didn't get to the room until five a.m. that morning. They must have had such a great time. I felt like such a loser. I kept looking at my phone to see if James had texted me, but he hadn't since the birthday text. Just one day into my thirties and here I was at some random café in a foreign city sitting by myself. I hoped this wasn't a foreshadowing of what the decade was about to hold for me.

I met up with the girls at two p.m., who were all now starving. We went to a nearby restaurant, and I watched them scarf down their food and talk about the night before.

"You really missed out," Payton said with a smirk on her face. It turned out she slept with Danny.

"Yeah, well, Trevor was all about you, Amber. And Kyle thought he was going to have a threesome with Erica and me," Mia laughed. I looked up at Erica, who rolled her eyes.

"About me?" I asked.

"Yes, he kept asking about you. If we should check up on you, if you had a boyfriend – complete buzz kill," Mia said, taking a sip of her drink. "He's definitely going to text you today."

I hadn't thought about that. It's been so long since I was in the 'dating scene'. I felt terrible; I didn't want him to think I was a tease.

"So, what did you end up doing?" I asked, changing the subject.

"We hopped around for a while, then ended up at the casino," Erica said. "They wanted to meet up again tonight, but I'm not feeling it, to be honest."

Payton looked up, disappointed. "We're not going to meet them?"

"I don't want to. You guys?" Erica asked, looking at Mia and me.

"I'm good," Mia said. I just shook my head. Payton looked down at her plate of food.

"You can go with Danny. We won't be mad," I reassured her.

"No, it's your birthday," she argued.

"Yesterday was my birthday. Today is just Saturday," I said. Payton made plans to meet up with Danny, and the three of us headed back to the hotel to get changed for the night.

"So, what happened last night?" Mia asked me when we got back to the room.

"Nothing, I had a headache."

"A headache, huh? Is that headache named James by chance?" She asked, raising her eyebrows.

"No, he has nothing to do with it," I said.

"You seemed like you were really into Trevor," she said.

"I was. Then we were making out and fooling around a bit, and I realized I wasn't," I explained.

"You realized in the middle of fooling around you no longer liked him? Did he do something wrong?" She asked skeptically.

"No, he didn't do anything wrong. I just wasn't feeling it anymore."

"And the lingerie you bought earlier, nothing to do with James either, right?"

"What is up with all the questions? Okay, yes, the lingerie is for James. What do you want me to say? I'm not into one-night stands. I never was. And as far as the lingerie goes, it's not like I'm going to run home and give it to him. I will wear it one of these days; he won't even know when or where I got it." I started brushing my hair.

"You're not into one night stands?" She repeated. "He was supposed to be a one-night stand, remember? What happened to 'one and done'?" I didn't say anything. "You're falling for him!"

I put the brush down. "What? That is ridiculous. I am not. We just happen to have good sex, that's all. *Really* good sex."

"Would you be mad if he slept with someone else?" She asked. I thought about it. I pictured him leaving the bar last night, some random girl by his side like I've seen him do so many times before. I felt a knot develop in my stomach but quickly dismissed it.

"No," I answered instantly. "He is very into safe sex, so at least I know if he did sleep with someone, he'd wrap it up." My phone vibrated. *Trevor.*

"Shit, what am I going to say to Trevor? He wants us to meet up tonight," I asked.

"Nothing, just ghost him," she said.

"No way. He was so nice, and they picked up our dinner. I can't be that mean!"

"What else do you suggest? You want to tell him you're sick for the next two days?" She asked. She was right. I had nothing I could say to him to explain why I didn't want to see him again. So, I simply wrote: *thank you for dinner. I had a great time. I need to spend some quality time with my girls, though.*

He never answered. Sure, I'm the nice one, and I get ghosted. Luckily, we didn't run into them again. Danny didn't end up texting Payton. I am pretty sure it was because of what I said to Trevor, but I didn't tell her that. The next two days, we did exactly what I told Trevor we would be doing. We had much-needed girls' time.

As I was packing up on Monday, James finally ended up texting me. *What time do you land?*

This time I answered back right away. *Eleven.*

Wanna come over? was his next text.

Sure. I responded and had the taxi take me straight to his apartment from the airport.

The second he opened the door, he was kissing me as he concurrently rolled my suitcase into his living room. I backed him straight to the couch and sat down on him without taking my lips off his. After a few minutes of passionate kissing, he pulled back. "How was New

Orleans?" He asked.

I smiled. "A lot of fun." I extended myself away from him, studying him up and down. He was wearing a backward baseball cap, with a white t-shirt and gray joggers. "I am so loving this look," I said as I ran my hands down his chest.

With one hand on my waist, he reached his other past me, retrieved a nicely wrapped gift bag off his coffee table, and handed it to me. "Happy Birthday," he said.

I took the bag from him and looked down in surprise. "You got me a gift?" I asked.

"Obviously," he said, still smiling. "Open it."

I climbed off of him and sat next to him on the couch. I reached inside and took out a beautiful box of perfume and lotion set. I opened it up and smelled it. "Thank you. It smells great," I remarked as I sprayed myself. He let out a sigh of relief.

"Good. It took me an hour to pick one out. I smelled so many different perfumes they all started smelling the same after a while."

He reached into his pocket and handed me a handful of cardboard samples. "Here are all the samples. If you like another one better, you can exchange it," he said. As I was flipping through the cards, I noticed one had a phone number handwritten on it. I handed it to him.

"I think this one is for you," I said, laughing.

He looked down, surprised to see a phone number on it. "Girls still write their numbers?" he asked, squinting his eyes at the card.

I shrugged. "Guess so. Why don't you call it?"

He flicked the card on the coffee table and looked back at me. "Honestly, I don't even remember what she looked like. Plus, I am busy at the moment," he said, bringing me back into him, and once again attaching his lips to mine. I started rubbing between his legs as he lifted my shirt above my head and unbuttoned my jeans. As I followed his lead, reaching my hand down his pants, he retracted from me suddenly and said:

"Oh shit, did we use the last condom last week?" He looked down, biting on his thumbnail as if he were trying to remember. "Yeah, we did," he said, releasing an exaggerated huff and standing up, repositioning himself in his joggers.

"You haven't had sex all week?" I asked, amazed. He ignored my question.

"You want something from the pharmacy?" He asked. I shook my head no. "Gatorade?" He suggested. I smiled. Guess he knew me just as well as I knew him.

"Yes, I'll have a Gatorade," I said. He leaned over and kissed me while taking my hand and guiding it down between my legs.

"Keep yourself aroused for me," he commanded, stepping back as he watched me continue to rub myself. "I'll be right back."

I didn't remember him coming back but woke up wrapped in his arms. As I slowly opened my eyes, stretching my neck, I realized I was entangled in him. He started opening his eyes. Our eyes locked for a second, and then he also looked down to see we were intertwined in each other's bodies.

"For the record, you initiated this," he whispered. I let out a laugh.

"Oh, did I?" I asked.

"Yes," he said, now kissing me and rolling me over on

my back. "When I came back from the pharmacy, you were passed out on the couch. Out cold; snoring, drooling, the whole nine yards. It was pretty gross. So, I carried you to bed. You opened your eyes for a split second to see it was me, and then your head was in my chest, your arms around me. I merely reciprocated," he explained, I'm sure embellishing his version of the story.

As his lips trailed from my neck, down my chest, to my stomach, I looked up and realized the scenery was completely different today: white walls, gray comforter, blue cotton sheets.

"Are we in your bedroom?" I asked.

Without taking his lips off of me, he mumbled, "You were too heavy to carry to the other room."

I smiled as his lips traveled down my body and until his mouth was between my legs. This man had an answer for everything. As he licked me, I felt as if I hadn't seen him in months. My body instinctively responded to his every touch. I felt so many different emotions. I was relieved I didn't sleep with Trevor, excited to be back with James. I realized I actually missed him. It somehow made sex with him that much more enjoyable and surprisingly even meaningful – even if that wasn't what it was for him. When we were finished, I sat up to find my clothes.

"Where are you going?" He asked.

"Home," I replied.

He pulled me down to him, arms around me, as he moved my hair to the side of my neck. I felt his lips nuzzle the back of my shoulder.

"Don't go. I haven't seen you in almost a week. Plus, I bought a box of twenty-four condoms."

I rolled around to face him, now my arms around him

also.

"Did you miss me?" I asked, feeling better about myself that I had missed him. He smiled and looked up towards the ceiling.

"Miss is a strong word. There might have been a small void."

"Who is this man I am with?" I asked, running my hands down his chest. "Cuddling, sex in his bedroom, having all the feels." He rolled his eyes.

"I was cold. You know, you're very observant – you should have been a detective or a reporter," he teased.

"Actually, I was supposed to be a reporter. My degree is in journalism," I answered as he rolled over on his back, and I laid my head on his chest.

"You missed your calling," he replied.

"Can I interview you?" I asked playfully. He looked down and smiled at me, running his fingers through my hair.

"Sure, go ahead," he said.

"Mr. Nisan, do you swear to tell the whole truth and nothing but the truth – so help you God?" I teased.

"Is this an interview or an interrogation?" He laughed. I chuckled also.

"How old were you when you lost your virginity?" I began.

"Fifteen," he responded.

"Fifteen? Jeez! Have you ever had a girlfriend?" Was my second question.

"No," he simply stated.

"Do you remember the night we first slept together? Do you remember what you told me?" I asked.

He tilted his head, looking up at the ceiling as if he

were trying to remember. "No, what did I tell you?"

"You said you thought about it for a long time," I reminded him.

He nodded, conceding he remembered it.

"How long?"

"How long have you worked at the bar for?" He asked me.

"Five and a half years," I said.

"So... five and a half years," he answered.

"Really? You wanted to sleep with me as soon as you met me?" I asked, my eyes widening.

"Amber, have you seen yourself? You're fucking hot – anyone with a dick would imagine it in you."

This was it, I realized. This was the time to address every rumor I've ever heard about him. I started running my finger up and down his dog tag tattoo and said: "Word around town is that you're a freak. Is it true you like to get girls to do things they normally wouldn't do?"

His eyes narrowed, and he let out a laugh. "Oh, is that the word around town? Yes, I guess that is true."

"Why?" I asked.

He continued running his fingers up and down my back, almost as if it was just natural. "When I was fifteen, I wasn't interested in girls. I liked sports, cars, comics, anything but girls. For no particular reason other than I guess I just hadn't matured to that level. My mom asked me if I was gay. She had this whole conversation with me about how it would be okay, and she'd love me just the same whether I liked boys or girls."

"She thought you were gay?" I repeated.

"Apparently. So, I asked Rob if he thought I was gay, and he asked me, 'well, do you like boys'?" He chuckled before continuing the story. "Later on that night, my parents were out, and Rob had a 'man to man' talk with me. He told me, if a girl really likes you, she'll do whatever you want. 'You know girls love being your first of anything'. Thinking that was a genius idea, Pete and I started using that line on girls, which one of us never got kissed or had sex, etc. Until I was seventeen, I had only had threesomes, me, Pete, and some girl wanting to be our 'first'."

"That is true; we do like being the first of things. Too bad I can't be your first for anything."

"That's not true; you're my first for a few things," he argued.

"Like what?" I asked.

He thought about it. "For starters, you're the first girl I had sex without a condom with. You're the first girl I slept with in my bed and the first girl I cuddled with," he said, bringing me in closer to him. I couldn't believe that after sleeping with him for almost six months, everything I heard about him was true. I had really written them all off in my head as rumors.

"Is it true you like to videotape?" I asked next. He let out a sigh.

"You girls really do talk, huh? Yes, that is true also," he answered, not taking his stare off me.

"Have you ever videotaped me?" I asked, nervous about the answer and suddenly looking around his room for evidence of a camera somewhere. He pulled back.

"Wait a minute, liking to videotape and being a pervert are two entirely different things! I don't have cameras hidden around the house. Any girl I have taped knew about it and was eager to participate. Completely consensual!"

"How come you never asked me to videotape?" I asked, strangely enough feeling a little insulted.

"I don't know. Just never thought to ask you," he answered.

"You don't want to watch me on video?"

As if my question aroused him, he buried his head in my shoulder and started to kiss my neck. "I would love to videotape you. You wanna make a video?" he asked, seemingly stunned I would want any part of it.

Normally he'd be correct, and I wouldn't have said yes to something like that in the past. But I wanted to get kinky with him at that moment and make a video, knowing he'd be watching me after I was gone. Finally, I understood why girls wanted to do crazy things with him. All of a sudden, I wanted to do whatever he wanted. "Yes," I whispered. "For research purposes, of course."

He took his lips off my neck and slid my hair out of my face. Then, he ran his thumb along my bottom lip and said: "It's in the other room. Let's go."

I put on his t-shirt that was thrown on the floor and followed him into the other room. I sat on the bed and watched him as he set up his iPad on a dresser to face the bed. He started adjusting it to make sure the angle was perfect. He looked so sexy playing with this device, only in his boxer briefs. I sat nervously, staring at him.

"Ready?" he asked, his blue eyes almost twinkling at me. I nodded. "I want you to look at the camera, not at me, okay?" he said. I nodded again, and he pressed the button to start.

I looked up into the camera. "Take that shirt off. Not your bra and panties; leave those for me," he instructed, the camera now rolling.

Still staring into the camera, I slowly started lifting the t-shirt over my head. I threw it on the floor and leaned back on the bed, trying my hardest to pose in a sexy position. He walked over to me and slid off his boxer briefs, and sat down on the bed next to me, leading my head between his legs. His hand guiding my head up and down on him, he started saying things like:

"Yeah, baby, you feel so good, deeper."

As he grew more aroused, he lifted my head and laid back on the bed, motioning for me to get on top of him. I did as he said, hovering over him as he slid my panties over and started massaging me between the legs with his thumb.

"You like that?" he asked, temptingly.

"Yes," I whispered.

He bit his bottom lip as he slipped one of his fingers in me. "You're so wet," he commented. "Tell me how much you like it."

He leaned up, took off my bra, and started kissing my breasts as he threw the bra to the floor.

"I like it a lot," I said, knowing that sounded stupid, but wasn't used to speaking dirty in bed. Especially with a camera pointed at me. He laid back again, reached into his night table drawer, retrieved a condom, and handed it to me.

"Put it on me," he ordered. I unwrapped the condom and rolled it onto him. "You want to feel me in you?"

"Yes," I moaned.

"How bad?" He teased.

"Very bad," I said, with a ridiculously pouty face as if I couldn't take the temptation anymore. He slid himself in me, and with his hands gripped tightly on my hips, led me back and forth on him.

"How does that feel?" He asked.

My brain scattered for something sexy to say in return. "You rock my world," I blurted out. He started laughing and slowed down his pace.

"I'm sorry," he said, still laughing. "What are we in the eighties? You want to sex me up?"

Now I was laughing too, still on top of him. "I think that song was the nineties." I laughed.

He tried to get serious again and sped up the pace of his pumping. "Give the camera a porn face."

I looked at the camera, biting my bottom lip and squinting my eyes in what I envisioned to be a 'sexy face'. But, I guess it appeared differently to him because he started laughing again and said: "That looks like a constipated face."

Now we were both laughing hysterically. He lifted me off him and rolled me on my back. "Okay, Ms. 'Color Me Bad', I'm taking over from here."

On top of me now, he thrust himself inside of me. Holding the bedpost, he pumped harder and harder, doing most of the dirty talk. Despite his attempt to be sexy, most of the time, we found ourselves giggling. I am quite sure not the type of video he was used to filming. He got the iPad and laid down next to me to view it together once we finished.

"I don't know if I want to watch this," I said.

"Why not? It's the best part," he said, pressing play.

I was so embarrassed watching the tape. It was far from what I imagined. We were laughing most of the time, and it looked more like we were playing a game than making an erotic video.

"I look so fat, delete it," I said.

He looked at me. "What? No way, you look hot. I'm not deleting it."

"I suck at doing porn, apparently. I look ridiculous," I argued.

"I think you look great! It looks like we're having a real good time. Isn't that what sex is all about? Having a good time?" He asked.

"I'm such a prude," I said, burying my face in his chest. He ran his fingers through my hair.

"You're not a prude; you happen to be great in bed. You are just more on the innocent side, inexperienced. It's one of the things I like so much about you – I think this is my favorite video. And you make a fantastic reporter!" He said.

I don't know if he was saying it to be nice or if he really liked the tape, but I didn't make him delete it. I was pretty sure he'd never want to watch it again, though.

"I'm starving," he said. "What do you have in that suitcase?"

"Nothing edible, just some clothes," I replied.

"Got a dress? Are you hungry? Do you wanna go to the steakhouse on Second? I can use a nice big steak," he said, now getting up and sliding his boxer briefs back on.

"You know how hard it is to get into that steakhouse?" I asked. He looked at me.

"No, I don't because the owner is one of my best friends. We'll get in without a problem."

"Are you asking me on a date?" I asked.

He let out an exaggerated breath and rolled his eyes. "No, I am hungry, and I am asking you if you want to go eat. Can't two people go to eat without it being a date?" He asked.

I sat up. "I do happen to have a dress that I didn't get to wear because the first night in New Orleans, I had to break up a fight between two of my friends. We didn't end up going out that night. Can I use your shower?"

"Of course," he answered. "I will text Andrew and let him know we are coming. Can you be ready in an hour?" I nodded.

After showering, I curled my hair, the same as I had months ago when he commented that he liked it, and wore a very tight, short olive-green dress with black five-inch stilettos. When I came into the living room, he was also dressed up. He was wearing black slacks, with a black button-down and dress shoes. With his dark hair slicked back and piercing blue eyes, he looked sexy as hell. I had never really seen him in anything other than jeans and a t-shirt before. He slowly looked me up and down, undressing me with his eyes.

"Damn, you look hot," he said. "I like your hair like that."

"Do you?" I asked, trying to sound surprised. "I don't know if you look better in joggers or dressed up."

"Not a fan of jeans, huh?"

I walked over to him and slid my hands up his chest. "Maybe I'm just used to always seeing you in jeans. You're looking sexy as fuck!" He smiled, and we made our way to the restaurant.

Chapter Eleven

His friend Andrew must have put his name on a reservation because we were immediately seated when we arrived. Crystal chandeliers hung from the ceiling, and beautiful flower centerpieces were placed at each table. There were mostly couples all dressed up eating at other tables. The brick walls on the inside and the fireplace gave it a very cozy and old-school feel. Being a very romantic spot, I couldn't help but wonder how many other girls James had brought there.

"So, tell me about this catfight in New Orleans," he said as we sat down. I started telling him about Payton's drunk incident as the waitress came over and asked for our drink orders. As I ordered a vodka soda, he ordered a Jameson neat and asked me if I wanted to share a seafood tower. I agreed and continued with the story. By the time the tower arrived, he was cracking up at Payton, vomiting all over my sneakers.

"I tried a charbroiled oyster and a barbeque one," I said as I reached for an oyster from the tray.

"The charbroiled ones are good. I've never had a barbeque one, though," he said.

"Well, we were actually only ordering the barbeque ones, but then this guy next to us suggested the charbroiled, so we got those also. I like the charbroiled better," I shared.

He looked up from his plate and folded his hands together. "You didn't mention a guy. Tell me about the guy," he said. I swallowed food and took a sip of my drink.

"These guys we met, we ended up going out with them. They were a lot of fun. But there were three of them and four of us, so they were outnumbered," I said.

"Or one was lucky enough to have two of you. Maybe you're not as innocent as I thought," he stated. I laughed.

"No, it wasn't like that at all. We were just hanging out with them."

"So... no one had sex?" He asked skeptically.

"Well, Payton did," I admitted. He let out a chuckle.

"Figures, the ugly one always gets laid," he commented.

"You're so mean! She's not ugly!" I insisted,

"Oh, come on. Yes, she is. You and Mia are by far the hottest; Erica's pretty sexy also. Payton, well she's...."

"She's just plain," I said.

"Sure, that's it," he said sarcastically.

"So, after that incident, we had a 'no shots rule'. But then Trevor started buying shots for my birthday...."

He cut me off. "Trevor, huh? So that was your guy?"

"My guy? I wouldn't call him *my* guy," I laughed.

"Well, three guys, four girls, who was he spending most of his time with?" he asked. I looked down at my plate. I didn't know why but I felt nervous all of a sudden.

"Me," I admitted.

"So, he bought you drinks. Did he ask for your number?" he inquired.

"Yes."

"Did you give it to him?" I nodded.

"Did he kiss you?"

"Yes."

The waitress came over to take our dinner orders. I ordered the salmon, and he put in for a steak medium rare. The second she walked away, though, James was back on Trevor.

"Was he a good kisser?"

I took another sip of my drink. "Why are you asking me all of this? You said you wouldn't care if I was with someone before I left," I asked.

"I don't *care*. We're just talking. I'm more interested in why you didn't sleep with him. If you were hanging out with him most of the night, and you liked him enough to give him your number *and* kiss him – why not go all the way? Was he a bad kisser?"

"I'm not that type of girl," I said matter of fact. He cackled.

"Not that type of girl? What type of girl is that? You're thirty years old and went away for your birthday. I don't understand why you would be afraid to sleep with someone you were clearly attracted to while in a different state. Who would even find out?" He continued.

I studied his facial expression for some sort of reaction.

He didn't look mad or jealous or even the slightest bit phased. This was merely a conversation to him. I didn't know what to say. I couldn't exactly admit I was thinking of him the whole time; that would just come off as pathetic. Locked in his gaze, I opened my mouth to answer, but thankfully the waitress came over and interrupted before I could say anything stupid. She held up a bottle of red wine to James to show off the label and poured me a bit to taste. I put the glass to my lips to take a sip. He didn't take his eyes off of me. The sweet, soft taste of fruit blended to perfection swirled around in my mouth.

"Wow, this is really good," I said. She poured me a glass, then James and put the wine in the middle of the table.

"Compliments of Andrew," she said to James. He looked up and flashed a fake smile at her.

"Thank you," he said. As she walked away, reached for the bottle and examined the label. "This is an expensive bottle; he must think you're special."

I watched him put the bottle back on the table and take a sip of his wine.

"Why does he think that?" I asked.

"He's never seen me here with a girl before. I guess he assumes we're on a date. Maybe Christopher isn't the only one who thinks I need to impress you," he answered. There was an awkward silence as we both looked at each other across the table. "So, why didn't you become a reporter?" He asked, finally changing the subject away from Trevor.

"Oh, you know, life got in the way," I answered as the waitress returned with our entrees. "My mom is very sick. She lived with me for a while. I was taking care of her," I explained in between mouthfuls of salmon. "She has Alzheimer's."

"Is that where she doesn't remember things?" He asked.

"Yes. A bad situation when you're living with someone. She would have violent episodes. She would suddenly have no idea who I was, throwing things, hitting me, screaming, and crying in fear. She kept thinking I was trying to hurt her. It got to be too much, and I had to put her in a home where people were..." he put his fork down and watched me intensely as I searched my brain for the right word. "Better equipped to help someone in her condition."

"How often do you see her?" He asked.

"At least twice a week," I replied.

"Does she ever remember you?"

"Sometimes, but not for long. The last time she did, it lasted no longer than three minutes."

"I'm sorry," he said sympathetically. "That must be really hard."

"It is. It's heartbreaking. Then, after that, I was planning for a wedding and needed as much cash as I could get," I concluded my story.

He went right back to his steak. "And now you're single, got a shit load of cash from a wedding you canceled, and still bartending. So, what's your reason *now* for not becoming a reporter?"

I was taken back by his bluntness. "I'm thirty with no real experience doing anything other than making drinks," I began.

"Sounds like an excuse."

"I have a one-bedroom apartment in Manhattan, and my rent is $3,500 a month on one salary now. You know what I make, I would never start at that as a new writer," I justified. Suddenly I felt myself getting defensive. All those years of Evan trying to make me believe I was staying there for James; did he think the same thing? That I was hanging around waiting for him? He scrunched his eyebrows as if he didn't buy it. Then it occurred to me – was I subconsciously staying there for him? My own doubt was making me angry. "Yeah? Well, what about you? You knew your whole life you were going to own a bar? What did you want to do?" I threw back at him.

He swallowed a piece of steak, took a sip of his wine, and looked at me. "Yes, actually, I did know my whole life I was going to own a bar. I just didn't think it would happen so fast. When I finished high school, I joined the army and got sent off to war. When I came back, I took the test to be a firefighter. I wasn't expecting my father to die a year after I returned. By the time I got called to the FDNY, I had already inherited the bar."

"How did he die?" I asked.

"Cancer. By the time they caught it, he was too far gone. There was nothing they could do for him at that point," he answered.

I looked down. Once again, I found myself being a bitch for no good reason. That was a terrible story. I looked up at him with empathy and said: "James, I'm so sorry. I didn't mean to...."

"Nothing to be sorry about. I am kind of immune to death at this point," and he went right back to his food like it was no big deal.

"So, this is it for you? This is your life? Playboy by day and bar owner by night?" I asked. He laughed.

"No, this is my life now. When I'm forty, I will buy a

nice big house in Long Island, have a few kids, and call it a day."

"Kids?" I exclaimed, stunned. "You want kids?"

"Yeah, why? You think I'd be a bad dad?" He asked, clearly having no clue why I was so surprised.

"No – I mean, I don't know. But how do you plan on having kids if you don't want a girlfriend, let alone a wife?" I asked.

"Oh, well, you see the way I look at it, most marriages nowadays end in divorce anyway. So, I'll just skip that step. I will find a girl who wants kids, and we can have an arrangement. I'll have them half the week, she'll have them the other half, and our lives won't change much. The kids will have never known their parents together so won't get damaged with a divorce," he explained, so seriously. His plan was well-thought-out.

"So, you basically want to be a sperm donor with joint custody?" I asked mockingly. He let out a laugh and pointed his finger at me as if I hit the nail right on the head.

"That's genius! A sperm donor with joint custody – yes, that is *exactly* what I want to be!"

We sat smiling at each other, drinking our wine. "Hey, I have an idea. What about if you're still single in four years when I'm forty – you can be my sperm's egg. I'll even pay the bills – then you'll have no excuse as to why you can't report or write, or whatever it is your journalism degree will get you." He looked at me seductively, "So, you want to be my baby mamma?"

His idea wasn't really that bad of a proposal after I thought about it. The best of both worlds. "Would we still have sex?" I asked.

"Well, I'm going to have to knock you up," he chuckled.

"May take some practice before we get it right."

"Okay," I agreed. "In four years, if I am still single, I'll do it. I can just see it now, me in the hospital screaming in labor for my 'significant nobody'!"

"I'm warning you, though. You'd be my first for that too; I've never got a girl pregnant. I'm not quite sure how it works; I may have to start with my fingers," he said, moving his pointer finger around on the tablecloth in a circular motion. "Try with my mouth...."

The waitress came to clear our dinner plates and hand us dessert menus as he was licking his lips at the last sentence. I had never been so turned on by a man without him even touching me. "I'll be right back. Let me go thank Andrew for the wine," he said.

I watched him make his way over to Andrew. Damn, all of his friends were hot. Andrew was his age, built, dark hair, olive complexion, green eyes – did they go to some sort of modeling school where they all met? I watched them shake hands and talk, then they both looked directly at me. I gave an embarrassed smile when I was caught staring at them, and Andrew smiled back and nodded as a silent *hello*. As I watched him speak to Andrew, I caught myself wondering what our kids would look like. I took a sip of my wine, trying to push the visual out of my head. Here was a guy who didn't want a relationship, and all I could envision was what it would be like to be the mother of his children. *He's unattainable*; I reminded myself.

When James returned to the table, he picked up the dessert menu. "You want dessert?" he asked.

"I do, but it's not on that menu," I said temptingly. Still incredibly turned on, I didn't know if it was the wine, the atmosphere, or his gorgeous blue eyes, but all I wanted to do was go home and let him do whatever he wanted to me. He smirked and signaled for the bill.

When the bill arrived, we both reached out for it, but he was too fast and quickly pulled it out of my hand. "I got it," he said.

"I thought this wasn't a date?" I said.

"It isn't," he replied, placing a few hundred-dollar bills over the bill and putting it back in the middle of the table. "But I make more money than you." He stood up and reached his hand out to mine to help me out of my seat. "Come on; I'll let you pick up the dessert."

Chapter Twelve

We practically ran out of the restaurant. He hailed a taxi, and I climbed in, anxious to get back to his apartment. He placed his hand on my knee. My body tingled when he touched me. I looked over at him. With almost no expression, he ran his hand from my knee, up to my thigh, and between my legs. He yanked my panties to the side and slipped one of his fingers in me. I looked up at the driver, who was too busy concentrating on the road to pay any mind to us. I stared forward at the driver through the reflection of his rearview mirror as James plunged another finger inside me. I had never done anything like that, and the thought of the driver catching us in the back turned me on more than I could have imagined.

As his fingers thrust in me faster, I could see him gaping at me and biting his bottom lip from the side of my eye. I straightened myself up a bit and spread my legs a little more. My eyes were still on the driver; my breathing became more complex as I tried my hardest to remain silent. There was no way I could let myself release in the back of that cab. A few minutes later, the driver had stopped in front of James' apartment. He quickly pulled a twenty out of his rubber band wad with his other hand and told him to keep the change.

He was fumbling for his keys as he had me against his front door, pressing himself up against me so I could feel how turned on he was. As I fiercely kissed him, he finally got the door open, pushing me against the other side as it closed. He reached for my leg and lifted it around his waist, his tongue wandering down my neck. My fingers gripped his hair tightly as he slid down my spaghetti straps. He stood back for a second at arm's length, slowly looking up and down.

"I have a problem," he said.

I looked at him, almost unable to breathe; I was so turned on. "What's that?"

"I'm not sure if I should rip this dress off you or keep you in it," he declared.

Then I remembered the outfit I purchased.

"I got you a present in New Orleans," I began. "Why don't you go wait for me in the room, and I'll get it for you."

"You got me a present?" He asked, smiling as if he knew it was going to be something sexy.

"Yes, go in the room," I repeated.

I watched him, curious to see which room he would walk into, and was pleasantly surprised when he chose his bedroom. I dug through my suitcase to retrieve the lingerie and quickly put it on. I left my heels on and strutted into his room. He was already in his boxer briefs, lying on his back. He slowly lifted himself up on his elbows as he watched me walk in.

"Holy shit!" He began. "You buy that for Trevor or me?"

"You."

"You are so hot!" He grumbled.

I slowly walked over to him and, as sexily as I could, crawled on top of him. I was rubbing myself against him, feeling just how turned on he was.

"You think that was nice? What you did to me in the cab? Teasing me like that?"

He shook his head slowly. "No, it wasn't nice at all."

"I think I might do the same to you now," I said, shifting the lingerie from between my legs so he could feel just how turned on I was against him. He groaned and stared at me as I teased him. I ran my finger over his lips until my pointer finger was in his mouth.

I started kissing his neck as he sucked on my finger and let my tongue wander down his stomach until he was in my mouth. My finger was now trailing from his mouth down his body. He reached down and pulled me towards him. I was now backward, perched over him so that he could pleasure me orally at the same time. I could feel his excitement grow, and just as he was about to climax, I stopped and turned back around. I continued rubbing myself against him again.

"How badly do you want to be in me?" I whispered, invitingly.

"Very badly," he grumbled.

"Beg me," I taunted.

"I want to feel you; I need to feel you. *Please* let me feel you," he pleaded. I reached into his night table drawer and retrieved a condom, rolling it on him. The second he entered me, he grabbed my hips, driving himself deep inside of me.

He watched me moving on him, mesmerized, taking it all in, and said: "Damn, you are fucking gorgeous, you know that?"

"You like it?" I asked, moving my body faster on him.

"I love it," he said, closing his eyes in pleasure.

"What else do you love?" I asked.

"You," he responded. His eyes flew open almost in shock at what just came out of his mouth, uncontrollably. "On top of me," he quickly added. My heart stopped for a second. Then he picked me up off him and turned me over. "My turn to take control," he said as he pushed himself harder into me, gripping my waist tightly. It didn't take long before we'd reached our climax, and I lay exhausted in his arms.

As I watched him sleep, Mia's words fluttered through my head. *You're falling for him*; she couldn't have been more wrong. I wasn't falling for him, I had already fallen for him. I realized that I was so in love with this guy at that moment, I now wondered for how long. Was I always? Was Evan onto something, being so jealous? I knew I was breaking the rules, but I didn't care. I wanted him so bad. Feeling this way about James made me ponder if I was ever even really in love with Evan at all? Or was he merely part of my 'plan'. Is that why I wasn't as bothered as I should have been by him cheating on me?

When I woke up the next morning, he wasn't in bed. I looked down and saw the ridiculous lingerie I was wearing. I slid out of it and grabbed his t-shirt off the floor, draping it over my head. I got up to look around the apartment for him. He was nowhere to be found. Memories of the night before waved through my head, and butterflies flew in my stomach. I loved everything about the night before. Going out with him, cuddling with him, waking up in his room. I loved being in his bed.

Reminiscing, I recalled the video we had made. I walked into the other room and sat on the bed with his iPad, now wanting to watch our tape. I envisioned how he would react if he saw me watching our video, how he'd like that I was enjoying it. I turned it on, and it asked for the four-digit pin. I put in his birthday—wrong password. I thought for a second. Then I put in the numbers on his tattoo, Jim's birthday. No match. Shit, think Amber. If I messed this up again, I would be locked out.

Suddenly a memory came to me from a few years ago. When we got the new safe in the bar, I programmed the password with my birthday. "Now, you can never forget my birthday," I had joked. I slowly typed in the numbers. 7 9 8 5. Score, the iPad opened. As I watched the recording, I couldn't help but smile. He was right; it was a nice video, after all. Watching how comfortable we were with each other, how much fun we were having, how turned on we both were despite the constant laughter.

When I finished watching it, he still wasn't home, so I exited out of the screen and went to put the iPad away when files appeared across the panel. There must have been a hundred files, all bearing different girls' names. My curiosity got the best of me as I pressed *Summer*. I almost dropped the iPad when the video came on. The things they were doing were so dirty; it was literally like watching real porn. His face was so intense, talking dirty and spanking her. I clicked out of it and pressed the next *Tiffany*. This one was just as dirty. I watched about five different videos; one girl seemed to get hotter than the next. He was so different in every video than he was with me. Serious, raunchy, *nasty*. My stomach suddenly hurt; I felt like I was going to vomit. I could hear the key in the front door as I quickly shut the iPad off, returned it to its place, and bolted back into the living room. He was walking through the door with a bag of groceries.

"You're awake!" He smiled at me. "You're in luck. I'm going to make my famous bacon, egg, and cheese omelet. Hungry?"

I stared at him, horrified. He looked at me for a second, his eyes studying my facial expression and his smile turned to a frown.

"Oh shit, you're Jewish, right? Do you not eat bacon?"

"I eat bacon," I said quietly as the vomit in my throat made an appearance.

I followed him into the kitchen. I dropped down in a chair as he started cooking. I felt so stupid. Here I was, head over heels in love with this guy, and everything I heard about him was true. He was a freak. I was just another girl for his video collection.

He turned around to face me as he was melting butter in the frying pan. I could tell he was wondering why I was so quiet.

"You okay?" He asked

"I don't feel good." Not a complete lie. I felt terrible. I felt like someone punched me in the gut.

"What's wrong?" He asked, now showing concern on his face.

"My stomach hurts," I said.

He came over to me. "Do you want something?" He asked.

"Yes," I said, now realizing I needed alcohol immediately. "Can you make me a Bloody Mary, please?"

His eyebrows lifted. "You're stomach hurts, and you want a Bloody Mary?" I didn't answer. I just looked at him with a stern expression on my face. "Okay, one Bloody Mary coming up," he said and collected the ingredients.

After making it, he placed it in front of me and said: "Sorry, I don't have celery."

I didn't answer. I drank half the glass in one gulp as he stared at me, astonished. "Should I make a pitcher?" He asked. I nodded. He started making a pitcher now while still cooking the omelets. By the second drink, my nerves were calming down a bit. He slid a plate in front of me and sat down across from me with his plate.

"You can add that to your list of firsts; I never made another girl breakfast before," he said. I took a bite.

"This is really good," I said, now focusing on the food.

He stared at me for a minute, and his chin rested in the palm of his hand. I put my fork down, and looking back into his blue eyes, I thought back on the past six months. He was different, and he wasn't that guy in the videos anymore, I decided. He bought me a birthday present, took me out, cuddled with me. He basically told me he loved me the night before, I justified. He told me the truth about the videos when I asked him; it wouldn't be fair for me to be mad at him now over his past. To be upset over a history that I knew all about before even sleeping with him would be insane.

"You seem deep in thought," he observed. "What's

going on in that head of yours?"

I stood up and went over to him and sat down on his lap, facing him while running my fingers through his hair. I whispered in his ear, "I think I want my breakfast in bed."

"Who am I to deny you what you want?" He joked as he picked me up and carried me into his room.

We barely got out of bed that whole day, and we must have had sex about six times. After, as we lay there, he ran his fingers gently up and down the inside of my thigh.

"Your hair is so curly," I commented, touching his curls.

"You kept me sweating all day, happens when it gets wet," he said, pushing his hair back with his hands. He hadn't shaved since I had been there, so his usually perfectly groomed five o'clock shadow beard was now rugged and shaggy.

"I like it curly," I remarked, running my fingers through it. "I like the unkempt beard too. Humanizes you a bit – makes you look not so perfect."

He gazed into my eyes. "You think I'm perfect?" He asked, pulling me in closer to him.

I shyly looked down and then back into his eyes. "Come on. You have a perfect nose, perfect teeth...."

"Took me four years of braces to get perfectly straight teeth," he explained.

"And those eyes! Where did you get such gorgeous eyes?" I asked.

"My mother," he replied.

"Your parents must have been really good-looking, having you and your brother."

He nodded in agreement. "My mother is beautiful. She was an actress, well, an aspiring actress. She came to New

York from Greece at twenty to pursue an acting career. But, instead, she met my dad, and they fell in love," he shared.

"Aw, she never became an actress?" I asked.

"No, but she didn't care. The best thing that could have happened to her was meeting my dad."

"They had a good marriage?" I asked.

"They had an insane, fairy tale type marriage. My father adored her, treated her like a queen. The biggest rule in our house was 'do not upset your mother.' They were crazy, madly in love – like dancing in the streets with each other, in love," he laughed and shook his head like he couldn't fathom it.

"That is so sweet!" I gushed.

"Sweet? Easy for you to say, they would embarrass the shit out of Rob and me," he laughed. "What about your parents?"

"Divorced when I was young. My dad lives in Texas now with his new wife and kids. They are eight and ten. Think about that one. I'm thirty; I could be their mother."

"So, it's only you taking care of your mom?" He asked.

"Yes, unfortunately, not much help there."

"I like your eyes," he said, pushing my hair out of my face to lighten the mood.

"Oh please, I hate my eyes. Who likes shit brown eyes?" I asked disbelievingly.

"Van Morrison, apparently. There's a whole song about it!" He said and softly started singing the words to "Brown Eyed Girl." I watched him entranced, thinking to myself in a million years, I would have never expected to be lying in bed next to James Nisan while he sang me "love songs."

My lips drew into his like they had a mind of their own.

"What do you want to eat tonight? You want to order something or go out?" He asked, slowly taking his lips off mine.

"I want to cook for you," I said.

"Cook? You cook?"

"Yes, I love to cook. Even nicer when you have someone to cook for. You cooked this morning, and now it's my turn. What do you have?" I asked. He sat up and stretched himself out.

"Not much," he said, leaning on the bed and looking down at me. "I'll take a quick shower, and you can send me a list. I'll go to the store."

"What's your favorite thing to eat?" I asked.

He fell back on me and kissed my neck. "You," he replied.

"That will fill you up," I specified, giggling.

"Whatever, I'm not picky. Surprise me," he said.

I texted him a list of ingredients and made chicken cacciatore. He really enjoyed the meal. As we were cleaning, he came up behind me and slid my hair from one side to the other to expose my neck, running his hands around my waist and kissing my shoulder.

"So, you're a great lay and an amazing cook. You better watch out; I may get addicted to you," he whispered in my ear.

Addicted! That was a perfect word; that's exactly how he had me – addicted to him.

The next morning, I woke up in his arms again. We didn't say a word; we simultaneously began kissing until we were both orgasming again. I think I had more sex with him in those six months than I had in my entire life. When we finished, I ran my fingers up and down his chest as he stared down at me.

"Are you going to hold me hostage again today?" I joked.

"I plan to hold you in many positions today, although 'hostage' wasn't one of them." He looked up to the side and tilted his head like he had just visualized the position. "Not a bad idea, though."

"I would love to stay longer, but I do have to go now," I laughed.

"You don't *have* to do anything you don't want to do," his rebuttal.

"I have to go to work."

He mischievously slapped my butt. "Yes, you do... go," he said, snapping himself back into reality.

I felt his stare as I got dressed. He sat up on the bed and picked up the lace lingerie from the floor, and playfully tossed it at me.

"Don't forget this," he said. I picked it up and tossed it back at him.

"That was a gift for you," I smiled. He took it and put it in his night table drawer.

"Best gift ever," he grinned. "I don't get a kiss goodbye?"

I walked over and leaned down to kiss him. He pulled my lips down to his and then whispered, "See you on Friday."

Chapter Thirteen

There weren't many people in the bar that night, as I caught myself constantly checking my phone to see if James had texted me. He hadn't, though. Looking up from a daze on my phone, James' best friend Pete was sitting at the stool in front of me. I hadn't even seen him walk in.

"Don't look so happy to see me," he said, noticing the look of disappointment that must have shown all over my face. I smiled and loosened up.

"No, I was checking something. What can I get you?"

"Coors light, please," he ordered. I took a bottle out of the refrigerator and popped it open, sliding it to him. "I've never seen this place so dead."

"Yeah. Thursday night in July, probably the worst time to come here," I answered.

"Why is that?" He asked.

"Well, New York City isn't exactly the summer travel destination. Most locals are headed down to the Jersey shore or the Hamptons. Even the Wall Street guys have summer houses," I explained.

"When's your busy time?" He asked.

"Picks up in the fall. Holidays are the busiest, Thanksgiving through the New Year, when the tourists are all here." He smiled.

Pete was definitely James' best-looking friend, in my opinion. He was tall and built similar to James, with brown hair, brown eyes, and a very neatly shaped goatee. He was dressed in jeans and a navy button-down as if he had just been out somewhere.

"Do you know where James has been? He meets me during my lunch hour every day at the gym, but he's been blowing me off all week," he said. I shook my head.

"No," I lied. "You guys work out every day?" I asked, changing the subject.

"Yeah, weekdays at least. If I didn't know him so well, I'd think he ran off with some chick and got married," he laughed, taking a sip of his drink. I looked down at my phone again, still no text.

"James married – now that's funny," I said.

"No, James married is not 'funny'; it's *impossible*. James and I have been best friends since kindergarten. He'll never get married."

"What do you do again? For work, I mean," I found myself once again changing the subject away from James.

"I'm a high school gym teacher and a soccer coach," he reminded me.

"Oh, right. I used to play soccer in college," I said.

"Did you? What position?" He asked.

"Striker."

He motioned for another beer. "You must have been good," he commented as I passed him another.

"Yeah, back then, I was good at a lot of things," I said, reminiscing my college days.

"What are you good at now?" He asked flirtatiously. I felt my cheeks get flushed.

"Apparently making drinks," I joked. "Which you clearly wouldn't know because you keep ordering boring shit."

He laughed. "Okay, make me an exciting drink. But you have to have one with me," he challenged. I smiled and started mixing us up drinks. I clicked his glass with mine and took a sip. He winced.

"Are you trying to get me drunk?" He asked.

"Sorry, I have a heavy hand," I said, shrugging. He reached out and took my hand in his.

"For a heavy hand, they are so small and soft," he commented. Looking down, I slowly pulled my hand back and took another sip of my drink.

"So, what's your story?" He asked. "What do you do for fun?"

I paused for a second and thought about the question. What did I do for fun? Well, I couldn't exactly say, "Fuck James." But, thinking about it, at that moment, it occurred to me I really didn't do anything much fun anymore. I was so wrapped up in planning a wedding, then canceling a wedding, taking care of my mom – and then this, whatever this *thing* was with James.

"I read a lot," I answered.

"Oh," he said, obviously unimpressed.

"I just got back from New Orleans for my thirtieth

birthday," I remembered. He seemed more interested in that statement.

"Girls' trip?"

I took a sip of my drink and nodded. "It was fun. It's hard having friends to do stuff with during the day, you know, working at night and all. I don't even wake up until the afternoon."

"I never thought about that. I guess that's true. Most of your friends have day jobs?"

"Yeah. I have a small group of friends who work nights. But our schedules are even so different it is hard to get together," I answered.

He slid the empty glass to me. "You having another with me?"

I smiled as I mixed the ingredients in the shaker. "Sure, but only one more. Can't get too drunk," I answered. He rolled around on his stool, looking around the bar. Other than a small group of three girls in the corner, the bar was empty.

"I don't think anyone will notice," he said.

Pete stayed at the bar for two hours. Although I had intended for that to be my last drink, I had four with him. He seemed like a genuinely sweet guy once we got into conversation. I hadn't ever spoken to him other than a quick *hi* here and there when he came in to see James. We had a lot in common. Aside from soccer, he was an astrology geek like me, and his grandmother also had Alzheimer's. He knew a lot concerning the disease and could relate when I spoke about my mother. A little after midnight, he looked down at his watch.

"I'd love to keep you company all night, but I have work in the morning. The deans hate when you show up hungover," he said.

"I'm sure they do," I chuckled.

"Will you tell James I came by when you see him?" He asked. I told him I would, and he left.

By two a.m., the bar was empty. The three girls who were there for hours had finally left—still nothing from James. I picked up my phone and texted him.

Haven't had a new customer in an hour. Can I close?

I was hoping he'd tell me to close and come over, but he didn't. He simply responded *OK*. I closed up and headed home, confused. I just spent three nights with him, and he didn't even text me after. Maybe I misread all the signals, and perhaps he did just love me on top of him. I laid in bed restless that night. Was he with someone else? Was I getting too clingy? Was he playing hard to get?

I was nervous to see him the next night, having no idea what to expect since he still hadn't texted me at all the next day. But, when he finally came in, he was in an exceptionally good mood—joking around and laughing all night. The same flirty James he always was.

"Someone is in an extra good mood tonight – you get laid?" Kaitlyn commented, not looking up as she made a drink. He grinned and raised his eyebrows.

"I *always* get laid," he answered and shifted his eyes to me. I wasn't sure if he was implying it was me that put him in a good mood, or he was trying to make me jealous by admitting he was with someone else the night before. I shot him half a smile and went on to help a customer. If he was, in fact, trying to get me jealous, it worked.

After Kaitlyn left and I was counting money, I felt his hands behind me, moving slowly around my waist as he kissed the back of my neck.

"I'm counting, and you're distracting me," I warned.

"Good, I like distracting you," he whispered in my ear. I turned fully around, now in his arms, as I ran my hands up his chest over his shoulders.

"Careful, it's your money I'm counting," I said.

He let out a sigh and said: "Good point. Just answer this, my place or yours, and I won't distract you anymore."

"Mine," I answered.

After having another mind-blowing sex capade, I laid on his chest with his arm around me. "It's hot as hell in here," he complained, half asleep.

"You want me to turn the air conditioner up?" I asked. He nodded as I got up to lower the temperature. Then a thought came to me. Did he say it was hot because he didn't want to cuddle? Being cold was one of the excuses he used for snuggling with me that first night. My imagination started getting the best of me, as my mind whirled with confusion. I laid back on the edge of the bed on my back, my brain still racing while looking up at the ceiling. He opened his eyes halfway and looked over at me. Then he rolled over, his body facing me, and reached out his arm to pull me back into him, wrapping his leg around me.

"James?" I said quietly.

"Hm?" He hummed without opening his eyes.

Slowly running my fingers up and down his back, I struggled for the words to come out. I wanted so badly to say *I love you*. But I couldn't. I didn't want to ruin what we had.

"Good night," I finally said. His eyes opened a little as he looked down at me, smiling.

"Good night," he whispered, his tongue slipping into

my mouth sensually. Pulling his lips away, he rubbed his nose on mine and kissed me on the forehead, drawing me even tighter into him. And that's when I knew: there was nowhere in the world I would rather be.

Chapter Fourteen

When he came in to work on Saturday, though, he wasn't his usual self. He was quiet and distant the whole night. He seemed distracted. I tried having flirty banter with him, but he was barely reciprocating. After Kaitlyn left for the night, I crept up behind him after I finished counting the register. He was doing inventory as I gently wrapped my hands around his waist from behind like he had done to me the night before.

"You're distracting me," he mimicked.

"Good," I replied.

Turning around, he slid his arms around my waist and under my butt to boost me up on the bar. Now perched between my legs, he started kissing me. Even his kiss was different. I could tell something was on his mind. I put my hand on his face, my fingertips gently massaging his scruff; "What's wrong?"

He looked down for a second and then back up to my eyes. "Nothing," he answered.

I slid my hand from his face to his chest. "I know you better than that, and something is on your mind. What is it?" I asked.

He placed his hands on my thighs, looked past me, and said, "I need to ask you something."

"Ask me."

He went to speak but stopped himself. He gave me an embarrassed smile. "I feel like I am back in junior high school," he said, letting out a small laugh.

He was nervous, I realized. He was going to ask me to be his girlfriend. My heart beat fast with excitement. I could feel the butterflies in my stomach again, and I wanted to be his girlfriend so badly. I ran my hands back up around his neck and pulled him closer to me. Our lips practically touching, I looked straight into his eyes.

"Ask me," I whispered confidently.

He took a step back and put his hands in his pockets. He glanced down at the floor for a second and then looked back at me.

"Pete wants your phone number," he said. My heart abruptly sank.

Startled, I asked, "You want me to go out with Pete?"

He looked over at the bar. "No, I don't *want* you to go out with Pete. He wanted me to ask you. We were working out today, and he said you guys had a great conversation here on Thursday night. Spoke for hours. He asked me if you had a boyfriend."

"Did you tell him about us?" I asked.

"No," he said matter of fact. "We agreed we weren't

going to tell anybody, remember?"

I wrapped my arms around my waist. "And how would you feel about that?"

He ran his hand through his hair and stretched his neck. "I don't care, do what you want. If you like him, go out with him. I'm not your..." he paused.

I waited for him to finish his sentence. To say what I was so sure he was going to say: *I'm not your boyfriend.* I glared at him, waiting for it. My thrill was quickly turning into anger. I felt so stupid. How did I let myself do this? I knew from the beginning he wasn't looking for anything serious. So why did I let myself fall in love with him? He finally broke the silence and completed his sentence,

"... keeper."

I'm not your keeper.

That stung even worse than boyfriend. "Oh, you're not my *keeper*?" I said, pushing myself off the bar, now standing.

"What do you want me to say, Amber? You want to go out with him, then go out with him. I'm not holding you back. We said this was just sex, right? Isn't that what you said you wanted? Rebound sex? A guy 'incapable of falling in love'? Weren't those your words?"

I felt my hand clench into a fist. It took all the self-control I had not to punch him in the face. It made sense why he hadn't texted me that night. He didn't care. Once I was out of his apartment, he probably didn't think twice about me again. To think I lost sleep over him! I shook my head in disgust.

"Fine, give him my number," I spitefully said.

"Fine," he quickly retorted and took out his phone. I watched him as he scrolled through his contacts. "There, he has your number now."

He turned back around to the other side of the bar and continued doing inventory. I walked back over to the register, collected the cash I had just counted, put it in an envelope, and placed it next to him. He didn't say anything. I waited a few seconds, still nothing. He didn't even look up.

"I'm tired. I'm going home," I said. He turned around and finally looked at me.

"You don't want me to walk you?" He asked.

"No," I began. "Don't worry about it. I'll be fine. You're not my keeper."

I had only made it a few blocks before I picked up the phone and called Mia. I just wasn't ready to go home yet. I was mad, ashamed – mortified that I fell for his bullshit— one of the many girls who fell under the 'spell' of James Nisan. I was so angry with myself; this wasn't me. I regretted not sleeping with Trevor in New Orleans. I was sorry I bought that stupid slutty outfit for James. I was growing angrier by the minute, so I was absolutely fuming by the time I arrived at Mia's place. "What's wrong?" She exclaimed when she saw my expression.

"Vodka," I said. "I need vodka."

We walked into her kitchen, and she made us both a drink. She was still dressed from the lounge, in a sexy black dress, now barefoot from standing all day. I sat down at the table, and she slid the glass to me, her eyes wide open, anxiously awaiting my rant.

"I'm gonna quit the bar," I said.

"What? Why?"

"So, everything we heard about James, all the rumors, *all* correct," I said.

She put her drink down and covered her mouth with her hand. "Did he videotape you?" She asked, her tone changing now to angry.

"Well, yes, but I knew that. I willingly participated," I said. "But I did find the ones of him with the other girls. Oh my God, Mia, the dirty things he was doing!"

"Like what?"

"Just like being rough, talking dirty... one girl he...." I couldn't even finish the sentence. The memory still repulsed me. Even so, she glared at me, waiting for me to complete my thought. "Let's just say he knows how to tie a knot, amongst other things."

"Did you ask him about them?" She asked.

"Yes, before I found them. He did tell me about them, confirmed it was all true."

"So, he admitted he made them?" She asked, now taking another sip of her drink.

"Yes," I nodded.

"Does he know you watched them?" She asked.

"No."

She opened her mouth to talk, then paused. She took another sip of her drink and leaned into me. "I'm going to be honest, Amber; I am a bit confused. What exactly are we mad about?"

"His best friend, Pete, came in the bar Thursday. I had just been with James for three days. Three days! I went there right after we landed that night. We cuddled, lay in bed, he took me to dinner – to the expensive steakhouse on Second. I cooked for him. Real couple shit! I even wore the outfit from New Orleans. Then I didn't hear from him. At all. Until he came to work Friday and made some stupid joke to Kaitlyn about always getting laid."

She was staring at me intensely, trying to understand where I was going with the story. I knew I probably wasn't making sense.

"Then tonight, he tells me Pete wants my number, and he doesn't care if I go out with him. Said he wasn't my 'keeper'."

"Do you like Pete?"

"I mean, he's okay, but you don't think this is all incredibly fucked up?" I asked.

"Which part? I mean, you and James did agree to a casual sex relationship. Do you want more from him? I mean, is he capable of even giving more? You did know what a player he was before you slept with him," she rationalized.

"But he's not really a player at all. He's actually very honest, funny, caring – incredible in bed...."

"Okay, I see what's happening here," she began, getting up to refresh our drinks. "You finally had good sex. He popped your prude cherry, and you're not ready to give it up yet."

"Hey, you said I wasn't a prude!" I protested.

"Oh c'mon, we both know I was lying. Of course, you were a prude! But Amber, you can't quit your job over this. For starters, you're breaking your own rule of no strings attached. Secondly, God only knows what he'll tell Rob. Rob is already the biggest douchebag I know, and that's him on a good day. I can't even imagine what type of dick he'll be if my best friend screws over his brother."

She had a point; she did get me the job. It wouldn't be fair to her if my quitting affected her job also.

I took the fresh drink from her and stared into the cup. Watching the little bubbles from the carbonation dance around the top of the drink as if it were some magical occurrence.

"You make a lot of money there. Do you really feel like you can't work with him anymore?" She asked.

"You were right. I am in love with him," I admitted, not looking up from my drink.

"So why don't you just tell him that? Maybe he's testing you with this whole Pete thing."

I let out a deep breath and shook my head. "No, Mia, he's not testing me. He doesn't feel the same way. I'm sure of it."

"Then I am really sorry, but these are the chances people take when they have casual sex relationships. Not to mention he is your boss; you broke like every sex rule possible. But you can't quit. Don't give him the satisfaction! Go out with Pete. Maybe James will realize then that he has feelings for you. And even if he doesn't, you may end up really liking Pete. The way I look at it, it's a win, win situation. The answer is easy: spite sex," she stated.

"Spite sex?" I repeated. "So, let me get this straight, aside from being a prude and maybe not experiencing things I should have, there are different categories of sex? Rebound sex, spite sex...."

"Hate sex," she jumped in. "Oh, maybe you'll have hot hate sex with James after this! Hate sex is always the best sex!"

"Is that even really a thing?" I asked, convinced she was messing with me at this point.

"Oh yeah, it's really a thing!" She laughed. Just when I thought I had learned a whole new world of sex, apparently, there was an entire dictionary I was missing.

Chapter Fifteen

JAMES

I heard her walk out and slammed my fist against the bar. Pete took me off guard earlier, telling me about their conversation. I had no idea what to say to her when she asked me if I'd be okay with them going out. I thought I had made my feelings for her apparent those last few days. When Pete asked me if she was seeing anyone, I wanted to admit *me*. Amber and I had agreed, though, that we weren't going to tell anyone. Evidently, they had spoken on that Thursday night for two hours. According to Pete, she was flirting with him and making him strong drinks, trying to get him drunk. How did she expect me to react to that? She had just left my apartment after a three-day-long cuddle fest. Listening to Pete brag earlier about everything she told him made me feel like such a dick.

I closed the bar and headed home. I was mad at myself. I should have texted her that night, but I purposely didn't. I wanted to a ton of times but stopped myself. I didn't want her to think I was getting too attached. It was against the rules; she said she didn't want that. It was supposed to be casual sex; I was simply a distraction to help her get over Evan. She said she wasn't looking for anything serious; then, suddenly, she's basically on a date at *my* bar the night before – with my best friend.

I lay in bed, trying to make sense of what had happened. *This is Pete; he will mess it up*, I wanted to assure myself. Okay, they had some stuff in common, but she would see him for what he really was and not be interested. He was the exact type of player she wasn't into. So, they'll go on a date, big deal. When he messes it up, she'll be right back here. Except now, maybe she would have slept with my best friend. My brain was literally arguing with itself. The smell of her perfume and shampoo poured out of my sheets. I stood up, ripped the sheets off my bed, and threw them in the corner. I pulled a pillow to me and tried to go to sleep, but it wasn't working. I could still smell the perfume. As if that bundle of sheets in the corner was tormenting me with the scent of daisies and strawberries. I got up and went into the other room. That reeked of her also. I took those sheets off too, gathered them all together, threw them in a laundry bag, and slept on the couch.

The sunlight peering through the windows when the sun came up kept me from sleeping as long as I would have liked. I got up and showered, and headed to the laundromat to wash the sheets. As I watched the load tumble through the glass door of the washing machine, all I could think about was going to the gym the next day. I needed to know if he texted her and if they were going out.

Finally, I picked up my phone to text Amber. It was three p.m., and she was already at the bar. We closed at midnight on Sundays, so her shift started earlier than usual. I held the phone in my hand, trying to think of what to say. Maybe I could stop this before it started. I racked my brain for the words; then, I hesitantly sent a text: *How's it going?*

Fine. She simply answered.

Busy? I asked.

Not really.

What are you doing after work? This conversation was getting ridiculous.

Don't worry about it, she answered.

Not worried, just starting convo... I wrote.

No need to start a convo..... we're good. You're not my keeper.

She was still mad. I shouldn't have said "keeper" that was dumb, but she still wasn't over it.

I'm sorry, I began to type. Then I re-read the conversation. I feared I was going to come off desperate. I deleted the message before sending it and put the phone back in my pocket while waiting for my laundry to finish.

"What does Amber like to eat?" Pete asked me the next day at the gym as he was spotting me bench pressing. "I'm taking her out Wednesday night. Any suggestions?"

"Sushi," I said, between breaths.

"She is so hot," Pete continued. I put the barbell down and straightened up.

"Pete look, I already told you this last week, but I feel

the need to reiterate. You better not do anything stupid with her. We have to work together. You better not...."

"Relax," he interrupted me. "I really like her, James. We have so much in common."

I rolled my eyes.

"Yeah, you told me all about it. You really like every girl a lot before you act like a dick. Just please remember, she works for me. I don't want any fallout, should you do something stupid like you *always* do," I stated.

"I'm not going to do anything stupid," he assured me. His eyes shifted past me as he signaled for me to turn around.

"Hi boys," I heard from behind me. I turned around to see Heather coming towards us. Heather was always at the gym the same time we were. She and I would flirt heavily, but I had never done anything with her. I made it a point not to sleep with girls who frequented places I did, so I wouldn't have to see them often. Heather was a lingerie model. She was stunning, stood about five foot eleven, blonde hair, blue eyes, and a body to die for. Completely augmented in every enchantable spot from her breasts to her lips, she looked like a real-life barbie doll.

"You look stressed," she said, pouting her lips, now approaching me. I started moving my neck from side to side.

"It's in my shoulders. I don't know what it is," I teased. She placed her hands on my shoulders and started rubbing her fingers down hard.

"Maybe you need a hot shower," she suggested, leaning her lips into my ear. "I can help you with that."

I turned my head, smirking at her, imagining steaming water pouring down our bodies. The thought was hypnotizing and not the first time I've had that same fantasy.

"I wouldn't know what to do with you," I joked.

"I think you'll figure it out. One of these days, I am going to give you a hands-on demonstration," she replied. She pulled her gym bag over her shoulder. "I have to get back to work, but now I have something to make me smile as they snap away." I winked at her as she walked away.

"You know you need to sleep with her already," Pete said. "This has been going on for years. What's the worst that happens, we have to find a new gym? There's certainly enough of them popping up in the city. I have a feeling she'll be worth it."

I laughed. "Don't try to deter from the conversation. Amber. You better not do anything stupid."

He shook his head. "I'm not, I swear. But, seriously, loosen up, man. What are you, her Dad?" I didn't say anything as I headed towards the locker room.

Thursday night couldn't come fast enough. I showed up at the bar ten minutes before she started. She walked in, surprised to see me behind the bar, swapping out liquor bottles. "What are you doing here?" She asked as she set her stuff down in the corner, preparing to start her shift. Without looking up, I replied: "My answer will never change when you ask me that question ~ I own the place."

She started cutting up the fruit for garnishes. "The health department is coming tomorrow for inspection. I just wanted to make sure everything is on point," I explained. She put the knife down and looked up at me.

"I always take care of the inspections," she said.

"And you still will. Two sets of eyes are just better than one," I said. She went back to slicing as I looked over and casually asked: "So how was last night?" The night before, I couldn't stop thinking about every move they were doing on their date. It drove me crazy.

"Good," she replied, not making eye contact. I moved closer to her.

"Good as in you're going to go out with him again?" I asked. She looked up and turned to face me.

"Probably. He's nice, and we have a lot in common. I had a lot of fun with him, so yes, we'll most likely be going out again."

"Where'd he take you?"

"The sushi place on Fifth," she answered. Of course, he did. That was the best sushi place in the area. I shouldn't have told him she liked it.

"Did you sleep with him?" I blurted out uncontrollably. She wrapped her arms around her waist in a protective position.

"How is that any of your business?" She asked, annoyed.

"Just asking," I said defensively, raising my hands in the air and backing up.

"Why do you care? You're not my keeper," she answered. I let out a sigh and rolled my eyes dramatically.

"Shit, if I knew that was going to be my tagline, I would have come up with a better quote for you," I said nastily. Realizing my tone, I inched back closer to her and softened my voice. "I was just wondering if you know...." I started waving my finger back and forth from me to her. "If *this* is still gonna happen, or if you have a boyfriend now."

Her mouth dropped, and she looked up at me as if she was appalled. She mimicked my gesture, waving her finger back and forth from me to her, and said: "That is never happening again, whether I slept with him or not. I don't bro hop. I am not going to go out with your friend, then sleep with you afterward!" I poured myself a shot of Jameson. That conversation went downhill real fast. I extended my hand out to her.

"Fine. It was fun while it lasted. Hope I helped you get over Evan," I said, now taking the shot with the name Evan. She reached her hand in mine and shook it.

"Yes, you did. Thank you."

"Cool, I'll see you tomorrow," I said, heading around the bar to go meet Christopher, which I was now late for.

Chapter Sixteen

"Sorry I'm late," I said as I sat down across from Christopher at the restaurant. We had dinner together every Thursday night at the same Italian restaurant since he was a little boy. The restaurant was nicely decorated with fabric tablecloths and framed pictures of scenes from Italy on the walls. It was small and low-key. He liked that he could wear joggers and sneakers there. We had been going there so long, the staff all knew us.

"I got caught up with something," I explained.

He took a sip of his soda and smiled, his dimple appearing. He looked just like his dad when he smiled. "Something or *someone*," he asked.

"Something," I elaborated as I studied the menu. I felt his stare on me. "Okay, something and someone," I admitted.

"Is it the girl from the bar?" He asked.

"Did you decide what you're eating?" I asked, trying to change the subject.

"Yes, the penne vodka. You?"

I scanned the menu. Nothing was calling out to me – I wasn't even hungry. I had lost my appetite.

"I don't know, maybe the chicken parmigiana," I said. The waitress came over and took our orders.

"So, the girl from the bar?" He asked again.

"Yes, the girl from the bar," I confessed. "I did something stupid."

"So, apologize," he said, simply. The waitress came over with a breadbasket and drinks. I started to butter a piece of bread.

"It's not that easy," I said.

"Why?"

"It's a long story. Enough about me, what about you – you still going out with that chick?"

"Jade? No, that ended months ago. I don't want a girlfriend," he said.

"Oh no? Why not?" I asked.

"I got too much going on between school, football, and helping Mom out. I don't need a girl tying me down right now. I'm kinda messing with this one girl," he said, scrolling through his social media to show me a pic.

He passed me the phone, and there was this pretty girl, posing incredibly seductively, with a shirt that barely covered her breasts and a tiny pair of boy shorts. She looked like she was getting ready for a Playboy photoshoot. I winced at the picture, suddenly feeling like a pervert for even seeing it.

"She's sixteen?" I asked disbelievingly. He nodded,

smiling at the pic. "My God, girls have changed since I was a teenager."

When the food came, I barely touched mine as he ate his. I asked him a lot about school and his football team, anything I could to distract myself from Amber. I couldn't believe she was going out with Pete again. I was obsessed with the thought of them having sex. I kept thinking about that guy Trevor she claimed she didn't sleep with in New Orleans. I really wouldn't have been mad if she had; it was just Pete that was specifically bothering me. Maybe because it was too close to home. Perhaps because I knew what a player he was, or maybe I would have cared if she slept with Trevor after all. My mind was still racing when we finished dinner, so I just went home and went to sleep.

Things got weird between Amber and me for the next month. Working so close together, and her still dating Pete, we didn't speak much. Anything I knew about her and Pete's relationship was from what he told me. She didn't offer any information, and I wasn't asking. This particular Friday night, things got very awkward after Kaitlyn left and we were alone closing up.

As she counted the register, I reached my arm past her to grab something, and it touched her slightly. She jumped so far back; it was as if a cockroach just crawled up her arm.

"Jeez, relax, it was an accident," I said, backing up. She straightened herself up and looked at me.

"Yeah, an accident," she said in a cocky tone.

"It was," I insisted. "Maybe Pete needs to touch you more often if that's how you react to human contact. You're getting weird."

"I was wondering how long it would be before you

brought up Pete," she said.

"You're quite the bitch today," I remarked.

"And you're a jerk every day, so we're even," she answered.

"Oh, I'm the jerk? You're the one who had a whole 'date' here the same day you left my house. Yeah, I'm the jerk," I said.

"It wasn't a date," she argued. "And you didn't even care enough to tell him about us!"

"Yeah, because we agreed not to tell anyone, but now you don't remember that part. And, no? It wasn't a 'date'? He knew more about you in two hours than I knew in five and a half years!"

"Well, maybe that's because you never bothered to ask me anything pertaining to some subject other than sex," she stated, getting louder.

I took out a shot glass and poured Jameson in. "And maybe that's because you were too obsessed with *Evan* to talk about anything else," I said, taking the shot at his name.

She came over to me, took another glass, and poured herself a shot also. "I wasn't obsessed with *Evan*," she said, taking the shot, "I was getting married and planning a wedding."

I poured another shot. "Yeah, planning a wedding with *Evan*," I took the shot, then immediately poured another. "Then who was there to help you when *Evan* cheated?" My third shot.

"*Evan...*" she said, taking another shot, "Was the only reason we even slept together."

"*Evan* was a pussy," now taking my fourth and leaning against the counter.

"Good thing you were nothing like *Evan*, huh?" She now took her third shot. She had this look on her face the entire time like she was trying to prove a point. Our argument, which had somehow become a drinking game, was getting intense. The more we drank, the more we hated each other. Then, finally, she shot me an arrogant grin. I leaned in closer to her, my breath on her face, and said quietly: "You're lucky you're Pete's girlfriend, or I'd fuck that grin right off your face."

She poured another shot. Leaning into me, her body now between my legs, she instantly had me aroused. Then she announced, "*Evan* was my fiancé. Pete is not. We are just dating. I am free to do *whatever* I want, whenever I want." She took the shot. Inches apart from each other, I pulled her closer to me by the small of her back, leaned down, and whispered in her ear: "Tell me what you want."

She tilted her head back so her neck was adjacent to my lips, then she stood on her tippy toes and put her lips right to my ear, laying her hand on my chest and muttered: "I want to make a sequel." She pulled back a little, so we were eye to eye, our lips practically touching. "Take me to your place. I want to make a video." I poured two more shots.

"To *Evan*," I toasted.

She smiled. "Yes, to *Evan*," as we both took the shots.

It all happened so fast. I don't even remember closing up the bar or walking back to my apartment. All I remember was getting through the door of my apartment and Amber getting very aggressive. She pushed me back towards the entertainment room, practically ripping my shirt off me, rambling something about "hate sex."

"Set up the camera," she commanded once we were in the room.

I started setting up the camera as she sat on the bed on her knees, slowly taking off her clothes. I pressed play and went over to the bed, and she pushed me down and got on top of me.

"I'm in control tonight," she said in an authoritative tone.

"That's quite alright," I said, smiling as she slapped me across the face.

"Shut the fuck up," she barked.

I held her back with my hand by her collarbone, and she proceeded to ride me. She placed her hand on mine that was around her neck and told me to choke her. My grip tightened around her neck as she let out a moan. She began talking dirty. Extremely dirty. Filthy. Usually, I would be all about dirty talk, but it just didn't sound right coming out of Amber's mouth. She continued, demanding I be rougher with her, saying raunchy things. She was a totally different girl than I once knew. All I could envision was her and Pete. Did he get her into this? Was this how they had sex? Was she this dirty with him? She certainly couldn't have been that way with Evan. And then she said something that would haunt me for the rest of my life.

"I want you to turn me over and fuck me hard, then pee on me like a whore." My body stiffened.

"What?" I asked, silently praying I misheard what she had just requested. She repeated it. I lifted her off me and sat up.

"Okay, I think you've had too much to drink," I began.

"No, I haven't," she argued, getting angry. "I want you to pee on me, James!"

"You definitely do not want me to do that," I tried pulling her down. "Just come lie down with me."

"Why won't you? I'm not good enough for you?" She demanded, getting angrier.

"You're too good for me. Come on, lie down with me, baby...."

"Don't call me baby! I am not your baby!" She cut me off.

I finally managed to pull her down to me in the spoon position. I held her in my arms. "Amber, please go to sleep," I pleaded. "You just need to sleep this off."

I ran my fingers through her hair and rubbed her back until she fell asleep.

When I woke up the following morning, she wasn't in bed. I got up and walked around the apartment, looking for her. I looked over at the couch where she usually left her purse, and it wasn't there. I went back into the room and sat on the bed, the hangover setting in. Rubbing my temples with my thumbs, trying to process what happened last night, I noticed the iPad from the corner of my eye. It was still taping. I went over to retrieve it and sat back down to see if it caught her leaving. It looked like she only slept for an hour, then got up and left. I watched her before she went.

She sat up in bed, looking down at me. I zoomed in to see her face. She was crying. Then shook her head in disgust before leaving me. I went further back on the video; did I imagine what she said last night? Nope, I was not dreaming it; clear as day, I listened to her repeat it. Pee on her? Where the hell did that even come from? I've gotten requests from girls for crazy things, but that was new, never had I had a girl ask me to... then I realized it. Yes, I did – *Veronica*. I went back to the files and pressed the name *Veronica*. It said *resume*. I never watched this tape after making it, but Amber must have. I went back on a few more. They all said *resume*. I threw the iPad to the side of the bed in anger. I sat there in shock. When the hell could she have watched these tapes? I went for a run to blow off some steam. I would have preferred going to the gym but was in no mood to be social. No matter how fast I ran, the anger wasn't subsiding. Drenched in sweat, I made my way to the closet bar and got drunk.

Chapter Seventeen

When I woke up the next morning, I was still mad. Furious, in fact. I couldn't wrap my head around when she could have watched the videos or why she even looked at them. I trusted this girl more than anyone in the world. I never treated her like a regular employee, and I always viewed her as a partner. I trusted her in my life, shared things with her that I would never talk about with just 'some girl'. I stayed at the gym an hour after Pete left. I was hoping to wind down, but even the intense workout didn't help much.

Before going to the bar, I stopped at another place a few blocks away and had a couple of drinks. I was trying to take the edge off before having to see her. I walked into the bar an hour later than usual, after I thought I had calmed myself down, but the second I saw her face, I was angry all over again.

"We were just wondering where you were," Kaitlyn said as I shot a dirty look at Amber.

"Can you come smoke a cigarette with me in the back?" I asked, frankly.

Her eyes were red and puffy, and she looked incredibly hungover. She looked down like she was ashamed of herself and went to her pocketbook to retrieve her cigarettes.

As we walked out, I lit my cigarette. "Anything you want to tell me?" I grunted, not able to control my tone. She held her hand up to her head.

"Please don't yell. My head is pounding," she said, lowering her voice. I stared at her, stone cold. "James, I am so, so sorry about last night. I was drunk, and I should have never made a move on you. It won't happen again – trust me. Pete and I spoke today, and we are now in a committed relationship."

I let out an exaggerated sigh and put my hand over my heart. "Oh, thank god! I am *so* happy for you and Pete! Really glad to hear you're going 'steady' or whatever the fuck you call it nowadays. That's what you're sorry about? Seriously? How about the videos you watched? You wanna talk about that? Did it turn you on, watching me fuck other girls?" Her mouth hung in shock, and her eyes grew wide like she had no idea what to say. She stayed silent, so I continued. "I trusted you – with everything! How could you do that? *When* did you do that? When the hell were you even in my apartment alone?"

She took a pull of her cigarette. "It wasn't like that. I was watching the video we made. I wasn't looking for them, and they came up...."

"When?" I demanded an answer.

"When you were at the grocery store."

I turned my back to her and started pacing the yard. Running my fingers through my hair, I turned back to her and said: "So let me get this straight – when I was out buying breakfast to cook for you, you were rummaging through my shit?"

"You know what?" She began. "I would sit here and apologize, but I'm glad I found those tapes. Do you know *why* I am glad I found them? Because it showed me who you really are! It didn't even look like you. You were a totally different person. Your facial expressions, the things you were saying. I guess that's the real you after all!"

"I never claimed to be anything else!" I shouted. "You asked me about them, and I told you the truth. I didn't realize you wanted a private viewing. You said you knew the 'word around town', right? Didn't you tell me girls say I'm a 'freak'? So don't sit here and act all innocent, like you didn't know what you were getting yourself into."

"You disgust me," she said, pointing her finger in my face.

"You made the move on me," I said. "Last night, and the first night!"

She put her cigarette out. "Do you want me to leave?" She asked. My pacing came to a halt.

"What? What are you talking about? You're working. No, I don't want you to leave," I said.

"So, you want to fight all night?" She asked.

I put my cigarette out and cupped my face in my hands. "No," I said, calmer.

"Then can we just pretend this never happened? Any of it. I'm sorry I looked at the videos. I shouldn't have; I was wrong. To be honest, I'm sorry I slept with you to begin with." I shifted my gaze from her—that hurt. "I never want to talk about last night or any night we had again. Can we agree to that?"

I looked down at the ground. I was now even angrier that she was somehow turning this on me, but I slowly nodded my head in acknowledgment to keep the peace. How she could just throw the last six months out like it was all a big mistake, when she was the one who betrayed me baffled me. I was genuinely speechless. I watched her walk back inside and suddenly understood the expression, 'you don't shit where you eat'.

The next two months were unbearable. We barely looked at each other, and we hardly spoke – unless we were chucking some sort of sarcastic jab at each other. Every now and then, she would throw in my face what a pig I was, and I would imply how untrustworthy she was. I contemplated hiring another bartender just so I didn't have to go to work. By the time October rolled around, and I was getting ready to leave for Vegas for Rob's bachelor party – I couldn't get out of New York fast enough.

Pete, Andrew, and I flew down to Vegas together to meet Rob and his two friends. His best man and business partner, Gary, and his friend Paul.

"When's the last time you were in Vegas?" Andrew asked as we were in the cab on the way to the hotel. The streets were crowded with people walking, traffic almost as bad as New York. The lights were glimmering off the casino buildings.

"I've never been here," Pete answered. I thought about it.

"I don't know, maybe like four years ago. Not a fan, to

be honest. I mean, honestly, outside of legal prostitution, what does Vegas have to offer that New York doesn't? They have good shows, big deal we have Broadway. You want to gamble, you go to Atlantic City," I said, unimpressed. Pete pointed at a group of girls, stumbling down the strip holding giant drinks in their hands.

"Public drinking," he answered. Okay, so you can drink on the street, big deal. As we went to get checked into the hotel, a guy around my age approached me. He was a little taller than me, very well dressed in slacks and a button-down, sporting a Rolex and diamond earring. He was very tan and in shape. I could immediately tell he was one of those show-off-type guys, it was only noon, and he was in a casino. Why he was so dressed up was beyond me.

"You must be James," he said, extending his hand. I realized immediately it must have been Paul, Rob's friend. Rob and I looked a lot alike. Despite the five-year age gap, once we were teenagers, I'm not sure if I looked older or he looked younger, but most people thought we were twins. The only difference was that he was usually clean-shaven, with brown eyes, not blue, and I stood two inches taller.

"What gave it away?" I joked.

"You look exactly like him," he said, knowing I knew the answer. "I'm Paul. Rob and Gary are meeting me down here to grab lunch. You guys want to put your stuff in your rooms and come with?"

I introduced Andrew and Pete and told him we would text them later to meet up.

Chapter Eighteen

After we got settled into our rooms, we headed down to meet the guys for lunch.

"Okay, here are the rules," Rob announced at the table. "Before Gary gets into the awesome activities that I am sure he has planned for this trip, there needs to be a disclaimer. No pictures, no videos, no tagging, tweeting, posting, as a matter of fact, no phones. We should all keep our phones in our room."

"Yeah, that's not going to fly with my wife," Gary jumped in.

"Or my girlfriend," Pete agreed, as I cringed at the word girlfriend.

"Okay, fine," he said, rolling his eyes. "You can bring your phones, but the original rules apply. We'll take some normal, nice group pics you can send to your significant others to show what you're doing. But after that, you know the saying what happens in Vegas...."

We all agreed and then listened to Gary's plans for the weekend. It started that night, at a steakhouse for dinner, then a club afterward. The following day would be filled with gambling, partying, eating at a nice restaurant, and private strippers in Rob's suite. The partying and gambling would then continue through the next day. Simple enough. That was just what I needed to get Amber off my mind. Until, of course, she came up at dinner when Pete asked Rob if he could add a plus one to his wedding reservation. He immediately put me back in a bad mood at the mention of her name. I intervened before Rob could even answer.

"Absolutely not," I simply said, in between bites of my steak.

"What? Why?" Pete asked, turning his whole body in his seat to face me.

"For starters, I won't be working all weekend and don't have a backup at the bar."

"I can have Mia work your bar, James. I have plenty of backup in New York. Plus, it will probably annoy her, which will be an added bonus to me," Rob offered, thinking he was being supportive. If only he knew how badly I wanted to punch him in the face for that proposal.

"See, Mia can fill in," Pete said, hopeful. "Thank you, Rob."

"Secondly..." I continued. "We are sharing a room, remember? I am not sharing a room with you and your girlfriend."

"James, we are sharing a *suite*. There will be plenty of room; bring a date," he suggested. Two single guys sharing a suite for a weekend for a wedding wasn't weird; however, bringing dates was just disturbing.

"Bring a date?" I said, shaking my head, horrified. "What single man brings a date to a wedding? It's like bringing a bag, already full of candy, trick or treating!"

Rob cleared his throat in an imposing tone. "You can both bring dates. James – you can have Mia for the weekend. Now, can we stop this bullshit and get back to the amazing weekend we are about to have?"

I thought about his statement for a minute. *You can have Mia for the weekend.* Now there was an idea; maybe I could bring Mia as my date? No, that would be too messed up. I couldn't bring Amber's best friend. Then again, she was dating my best friend... would it really be that bad? I snapped out of my thought when Gary announced we were leaving for the club.

Gary was Rob's business partner in Miami and had a lot of connections. I don't know how he scored a VIP table at the club, but he did. There was no waiting in line; we were escorted straight to the table. There were full bottles of Grey Goose, Johnny Walker, Jameson, Sapphire, Bacardi, and a few pitchers of mixers, laid out with buckets of ice. We even had a personal bouncer for the table. The club was packed; flashing lights illuminated the room, and the drumming of music beat through the floors. Girls were hanging from the ceiling, Cirque du Soleil style, only stripping while doing acrobatics. Perhaps Vegas did have a step up on New York when it came to the talent of their strippers. Rob, Pete, and Gary descended to dance with some girls as Paul, Andrew and I sat at the table drinking.

I poured myself another Jameson. "What are you guys having?" I asked.

"Comes in handy to travel with bartenders," Andrew laughed. "I'll have a gin martini."

"As if Rob would ever make a drink himself anymore," I remarked as I started making Andrew's drink. "Paul?"

"I'll make it easy on you; I'll just do a vodka martini," he answered.

"Feel free to get as fancy as you like. I'm up for the challenge," I dared.

He let out a laugh. "A vodka martini is fine for now; maybe I'll test out your mixology skills later."

I made them both drinks, and we sat there drinking for a while. Andrew left to talk to a girl, as Paul and I scoured the room for candidates. My attention was instantly drawn to a red-headed girl in a tight black dress, her hair curled, perfect-sized breasts, not too big or too small. Just as I was about to call dibs on her, I realized she reminded me too much of Amber. If not for anything else, it confirmed I had a specific type. As I leaned forward to get up to make my way over to her, it occurred to me if Pete caught me leaving with her, he may suspect what happened between his girlfriend and me. I sat back again and continued past her until I saw a brunette dancing with her blonde friend. Both dressed very seductively and aged probably in their mid-twenties; either one would do. Both would be better. I pointed over at them.

"I think I'm going for that," I shouted over the music to Paul. His eyes shifted to them, and then he nodded approvingly.

"Which one?" He asked.

"Whichever, they're both hot," I answered. "How about you? What are you looking at?"

He scanned the room. "I don't know," he said.

"What about her?" I asked, pointing at an attractive girl dancing with her friends. He shook his head no. I pointed at another pretty girl. He shook his head again. I must have aimed at five girls, none of which met his approval. "Damn, what is your type?" I asked. Once again, his eyes shopped around the room.

"There," he said, pointing at a girl with purple hair, a tight black mini skirt, and a cropped shirt displaying the tattoos she had on each of her rib cages. She was probably around my age and talking to a guy who looked ten years older than her. He was clean-cut, prim, and proper with thick dark-rimmed glasses, but with his sleeves rolled up, you could see his arms were covered in tattoos as well.

"She's cute," I commented, taking a sip of my drink.

"I'm not talking about her. I'm talking about him," he said. I put my drink down and let out a laugh.

"Yeah, okay," I said. He looked at me straight in the face.

"He's got that hot older Professor look, no?" He asked.

"You're serious? You're gay?" I asked, stunned.

He nodded. "Yup."

"No way," I said, picking my drink back up and taking another sip.

"James, I'm gay," he reiterated.

"You are not gay," I insisted. He took a sip of his drink and rolled his eyes. I turned around and looked straight at him in shock. I truly believed he was kidding; he didn't come off gay at all.

"Bro, I'm as gay as they come," he said, so seriously.

"Okay, see, right there! You called me 'bro' If you were gay, you would have called me 'honey', or 'sweetheart', something else – but definitely not 'bro'," I explained.

He blinked his eyes dramatically and pinched his lips together. "Well, that's quite the stereotype. I can't say 'bro' because I'm gay?"

Realizing he was serious now, I took another sip of my drink. "Look, I don't care that you're gay, just surprised, that's all. You haven't even hit on me once."

Now he started laughing. He leaned in closer to me and said: "I haven't hit on you because I am not attracted to you."

"What?" I asked, offended. "Why aren't you attracted to me?"

"Look, you're gorgeous, and you know it. If you wanted to be a model, you could easily get a job. But that's just it. You *know* it. You're cocky, arrogant, narcissistic...."

"Hey! You don't even know me – narcissistic? Who's stereotyping who now?" I cut him off.

"I know your type. When was the last time you had a girlfriend?" He asked.

"I've never had a girlfriend."

"Oh, even better," he said. "You haven't had a girlfriend because A, you either think you're always going to do better than the girl you've met, or B, you're scared. You don't strike me as the type of guy who frightens easily, so – narcissist."

I looked down, annoyed. "That's not true."

"I bet you have a big dick, too, right?" He asked.

"Okay, now I believe you're gay. No straight guy would ask that," I said, laughing, going back to my drink.

"Well, do you?"

"It's sizeable," I said confidently. I turned my whole body to face him. "And knowing that, you're still not interested in me?"

He shook his head, laughing, and drank the rest of his drink. "This is precisely what I mean. You would rather sit here with me all night, trying to convince me to like you, knowing full well you would never hook up with a man – just to satisfy your ego. Instead of easily going to one of those girls you were interested in before and getting them to go back to your room with you within no time."

"Sure, that's what I am doing. And I'm the narcissist!" I snapped sarcastically. "Not everything is about you, Paul."

"What's her name?" He asked.

"Who's name?"

"The girl you're thinking about right now," he clarified. "It's not about me, right? Well then, who is it about?"

"I'm not thinking about anyone," I said defensively.

"Then why are you still sitting here with me, exploring the depths of our sexuality?"

I put my glass down on the table and rolled my eyes. I stood up and straightened out my shirt. I looked down at my watch; it was only midnight. "The brunette, one hour," I estimated. He smiled.

"Go for yours, man. You Nisan guys have some severe head issues," he added, still amused.

I made my way towards the girls. Head issues? Rob was a genius! He had a good-looking wingman that didn't like girls, and there could never be any competition between them. Just when I thought I couldn't idolize my brother any more than I already had, he proved me wrong. It took an hour and a half, and it was the blonde I ended up taking back to the room. I hooked up twice that weekend, and it was just what I needed.

Chapter Nineteen

"So, did you decide if you're bringing a date to the wedding yet?" Pete asked as we were working out that Wednesday.

"Yes," I said, as my eyes searched the room for Heather. When I spotted her on a treadmill, I motioned over with my head. Pete looked over, then smiled at me.

"About time, my boy! Great choice," he said as I made my way to the empty treadmill next to Heather.

"Hey you," she said as I started the treadmill up.

"Hey," I smiled. "I don't typically use treadmills, but you make it look like fun."

She accelerated her machine and quickened her pace. "Wanna race?"

I put up the speed on mine, and soon we were running. We ran in place for fifteen minutes when she stopped her machine and jumped off. She came over to mine as I was still running.

"I must admit I prefer watching you bench press. You don't get sweaty enough when you run," she commented. I slowed my speed down until I gradually came to a stop. I strategically leaned my arms on the hand rest, feeling my biceps harden. I leaned towards her and gazed deep into her eyes.

"Do you want to have dinner with me tomorrow night?" I asked. She tilted her head and looked at me in surprise.

"I've been waiting long enough for you to ask me out. I would love to have dinner with you," she replied. We exchanged numbers, and I made my way back over to Pete.

"Woah, did I just watch you get a phone number?" He asked, amazed.

"Yes, we're having dinner tomorrow night. However, she needs to pass a few tests before I invite her on a weekend trip to Miami," I answered.

"Such as?"

"Well, I have to make sure I can have a conversation with her, and she can handle her alcohol. Also, got to test the goods before I commit myself to a whole weekend with her, if you know what I mean," I said, winking.

The next night I met her at a tapas restaurant she picked out. She was wearing a tight red dress that came down right below her butt and made her enormous chest look that much more prominent. She stood about an inch taller than me in heels, which made me feel a little awkward.

"Did you have to wear heels?" I joked as we sat down.

She twirled her hair through her fingers and shot me a smile.

"You clean up nice," she commented.

Wearing jeans and a button-down shirt, I realized she had only seen me before in gym clothes. She was a very picky eater, which made it hard to share tapas plates. She didn't eat seafood or meat, so the six dishes were all vegetable-based or potatoes in front of us. I was still hungry by the time we headed out to another place.

We didn't have much in common to talk about. She was originally from the South and only moved to New York a few years before to follow her modeling career. She wasn't into sports or movies or anything that I was talking about. She was extremely self-centered, mainly speaking about herself and her social media accounts. She made it a point to show me how many followers she had as if that were something I should be impressed with.

We went to a club afterward for a while, and once we had good buzzes, the night became more tolerable. We spent most of the time on the dance floor, so we didn't have to speak much. She was a good dancer and held her alcohol well, confirming the first two parts of my test. Conversation and alcohol covered, now for the third. After the club, we went to a bar nearby and had some more drinks. It was almost two a.m. and the nightlife was dying down. Most bars were already calling the last call when Amber texted me if she could close. I had responded yes until Heather was getting annoyed at the bars closing early.

"This is the fucking city that never sleeps! How are you closing at two a.m?" she complained to the last bartender.

"I have alcohol at my apartment," I suggested, trying not to ruin the mood.

"I want to stay out a bit, maybe play a jukebox," she whined. I texted Amber to stay open.

"I know a place," I said, grabbing her by the hand and hailing a cab.

"Does it have a jukebox?" She asked. I nodded, and we made our way to my bar.

When we walked in, the place was completely dead. Amber was leaning on the bar looking at her phone, then slowly straightened herself up when Heather and I sat down. Her mouth twitched a little, and her eyes widened as she slowly eyed Heather up and down.

"We'll have a Jameson neat and a grey goose and soda," I ordered as Heather rushed to the jukebox to pick out music. Amber made the drinks and slid them over as Heather returned, moving her body to the music she picked.

"Heather, this is Amber. Pete's girlfriend," I introduced the two as she took a sip of her drink.

"Hi, Amber!" Heather exclaimed. Amber threw a phony smile in her direction and looked over at me.

"Is there anything in the kitchen to eat?" I asked, almost under my breath. "Bread or something?"

"You want pretzels?" she asked.

"Anything," I pleaded, now feeling like I hadn't eaten in a week.

She went in the back and returned with a bag of pretzels she poured into a bowl. Heather ordered her second drink already, rubbing her body into me in sync with the music.

As I practically inhaled the pretzels, Amber watched as Heather seductively moved her body against my lap from behind. Finally, she turned around to face me, running her hands down my chest, still moving to the music, and pulled my legs apart to nestle herself between them. She ran her hands back up my chest until she held my face and positioned it in Amber's direction.

"Doesn't he have the most gorgeous eyes you've ever seen?" She asked.

Unamused, Amber looked into my eyes as she rolled hers. I knew what she was envisioning as if I could read her mind. The same thing I was when Heather asked her the question. Lying in bed with me, in my arms, asking me where I had gotten my eyes from. The same day I sang "Brown Eyed Girl" to her.

"Very pretty," she reluctantly said.

I turned my face back to Heather.

"You know what I like even more than your eyes?" She asked.

"What's that?"

"Your hands," she said, running her fingers through mine and pulling my hand up in hers. "You have such big, manly hands," she continued. Amber cleared her throat.

"James, can I talk to you outside for a second? Smoke a cigarette with me?"

"Sure," I said, following her to the yard while Heather stayed behind. Still dancing in place to the music, she was completely oblivious.

"Okay, this is really weird," she proclaimed as she lit a cigarette. "This girl is all over you."

"Jealous?" I asked, lighting my cigarette.

"Don't flatter yourself. I feel like I'm a third wheel."

I backed up. "A third wheel?" I chuckled. "No, Amber, you're not a third wheel. You're a bartender. Would you feel so 'weird' if some other dude came in here on a date?"

She flicked the ashes from her cigarette and looked up at me in surprise. "Date? Is that what this is? A date?" She asked, agitated.

"Yes, it's a date. If this is weird for you, imagine how awkward it is going to be when we're all sharing a room in Miami," I said.

"You're taking her to Miami?" She exclaimed.

I could tell she was bothered, but for some reason, I enjoyed watching her aggravated for a change.

"Look, I called every hotel on South Beach. There is a...."

"Convention – I know, I also called," I said.

"So, this is your solution to an already uncomfortable situation? You're bringing her?" She asked again.

"Probably. Or maybe I should take Mia – what do you think about that? Mia can be my date, and then we'll both have our best friends with us. One big, bestie party!"

She let out a scoff. "You wish! Mia would never go with you."

"You don't think so? That sounds like a challenge to me," I said mockingly.

"Mia would never hook up with someone I did," she explained.

I took another pull of my cigarette. "Mia knows we hooked up?" There was a silence as she looked down to the ground. "You are un-fucking-believable! You told Mia, meanwhile, I couldn't say anything to Pete when he asked?" I said, raising my voice. I was now livid.

"It wasn't like that. When I got back to my apartment that day, Evan was still there, and I went to Mia's...."

I shook my head, not wanting to hear anything else as I put my cigarette out.

"You know, you girls are worse than guys with your mouths. We promised not to tell anybody, but you told

Mia, and I didn't admit it to Pete. Yet somehow, I was still the jerk for *not* telling Pete. Is there something I am missing, or do I understand this correctly?"

She just stood frozen, still not saying anything.

"Whatever," I said, throwing my hand up in the air and walking away from her. "Oh, by the way," I continued, now turning back towards her again. "Should I drop my luggage off before we board the plane, or do you want to wait until I'm not in the room to dig through my shit?"

She threw her cigarette on the floor. "Fuck you, James."

"You already did," I hissed, blowing her a kiss and walking back inside. Heather was still dancing by herself at the bar, seemingly having no idea what had just transpired outside. Amber followed me inside and went back behind the bar.

As I sat on the stool, Heather put her arms around my shoulders and whispered in my ear: "If this girl weren't here right now, I'd let you have me right on this bar."

I looked into her eyes. "Is that so?" I asked.

She slowly nodded her head and kissed me gently on the lips. I could feel Amber glaring at me as I kissed her back. I gradually pulled my lips off Heather's.

"You can go," I announced, looking at Amber. Her face dropped, and she clenched her jaw.

"Are you serious?" She asked. "I didn't even close out the register."

"I'll do it," I said. With my eyes still on Heather, I wouldn't even look over at Amber. I ran my hands down Heather's back to her behind, pulling her in closer to me. Amber grabbed her pocketbook and stormed out. I got up and followed her out to lock the door.

"Have a great time," she said nastily.

"I am sure I will. I appreciate your concern, though," I said, finally making eye contact with her. I locked the door behind her and headed back over to Heather. I wrapped my hands around her waist, boosted her up on the bar, and started kissing her. "Where were we?" I quietly asked.

"Do you own this bar?" She realized as her fingers ran through my hair, and she pulled my face into her chest. Had she asked me anything about me on our date, perhaps she would have already known that.

"I do," I admitted.

Just as she promised, she let me have her right on the bar. When we finished, I stood between her legs, kissing her neck. She successfully passed the third test. "Do you want to come to a wedding in Miami with me in two weeks?"

"Miami?" She asked, surprised.

"Yes, my brother is getting married, and I need a date. I will pay for your plane ticket. We are leaving Thursday night and coming back Monday morning. There's only one caveat," I explained.

"What's that?"

"We're sharing a room. A suite, with Pete and Amber." She smiled and pulled me into her.

"I'm down," she said.

Chapter Twenty

Luckily, I could change our seats on the flight down, so Heather and I weren't sitting near Amber and Pete. Once we had landed, though, we were all packed in a cab in the pouring rain. I could see Amber checking me out from the side of her eye. Okay, I'll admit it, I purposely wore gray joggers and a white t-shirt with a backward baseball cap, remembering she said she 'loved the look'. I turned my hat forward as we got out, the girls sprinting to the hotel to try and avoid getting drenched, as Pete and I collected the luggage.

The minute we walked through the door of the hotel, I made my way to the front desk to plead for another room. Any room, I didn't even care if it was a closet. Still, though, nothing was available. When we got to the suite, fortunately, it was tremendous. You walked through a decent size kitchen to an enormous living room with a pull-out couch. There were sliding doors in the living room, reaching our private balcony with a table, four chairs, and a hot tub. It was probably a gorgeous view if it wasn't raining so hard. Past the living room was the master bedroom, with a queen-sized bed attached to the bathroom. The bathroom was large as well, with marble counters and a glass shower.

"We get the bedroom," I said, so sternly, no one dared to argue.

After unpacking our things and getting dressed, the four of us made our way to a nice Cuban restaurant a few blocks away. Heather and I were seated across from Pete and Amber. Spanish music played softly, offering a nice change from the crazier nightlife going on outside. After taking our drink orders, Pete thought he was cute, saying "Gracias" to the waiter like he was suddenly bilingual. I felt nauseated when Amber giggled and flipped her hair at him flirtatiously as if that was so impressive. After we ordered drinks, we started calling out appetizers for the table, but aside from Heather not eating anything that didn't contain a vegetable, Pete refused to eat seafood. Needless to say, it wasn't the easiest group when it came to sharing.

"I want the ceviche and the shrimp mofongo," Amber said. "I'm starving, and everything looks so good!"

"I'll share it with you," I offered. Pete looked up at Heather.

"Can you eat guacamole? I will share that with you."

She agreed, and Pete stood up. "Here, James, swap seats with me so we can share food easier."

"I'm fine here," I said, not moving.

"No, no, come here. You and Amber are sharing appetizers, and it will be easier if you're sitting next to each other," he insisted.

Reluctantly, I got up and sat next to Amber. She was wearing a tight short blue sundress and sandals. From the corner of my eye, I could see her lifting her dress a little to scratch her thigh. Suddenly all I could imagine was being in that cab with her, seated right next to her. Same scenario as we were then, running my fingers up her thigh before slipping them into her.

Now I was turned on, great. All I could envision was doing the same to her at that table. Right there, underneath the white tablecloth, across from Pete and Heather. I found myself mentally measuring the tablecloth to my lap and wondering if I could get away with it without either of our dates seeing. Then, staring at the gap between the tablecloth and my lap, I immediately started thinking about how she'd react. Would she jump up and make a scene? Or would she spread her legs a little more, like she had done that night?

"James?" Heather broke me out of my fantasy. "Is that cool?" I looked up at Pete across from me. They were all staring at me.

"I'm sorry, what?" I asked, realizing I had no idea what anyone was talking about.

"Pete and I want to go for a run on the beach tomorrow morning. Unless you want to come, but I know you don't get up that early."

"Yeah, I don't care," I answered as the appetizers were placed in front of us. Amber unfolded her napkin and put it on her lap, and there I was, right back to my imagination.

"Can I have another Jameson?" I asked the waitress.

One minute I hated this girl and didn't even want to sit next to her, and the next, I couldn't stop picturing my hands on her. She drove me crazy, to say the least.

"What is wrong with you tonight?" Amber asked, turning her head to look directly at me.

"Me? Nothing," I said, filling one of my chips with ceviche. "Just wondering how Mia is doing at the bar."

"She'll be fine. She's a better bartender than I am," she reasoned.

"So, the rehearsal dinner is tomorrow?" Heather asked me. I nodded.

"You have a rehearsal dinner?" Amber asked in a tone that I couldn't tell if she was jealous or surprised.

"Yeah, I'm in the bridal party."

"We'll do our own thing, babe," Pete said. She smiled, reassured. *Babe?* Give me a break.

After a few more drinks, my taxicab distractions were at bay, and we could hang out the rest of the night effortlessly.

When I woke up the next morning, the room was empty. Half asleep, I wandered towards the bathroom. The second I opened the door, Amber shrieked from the shower.

"I'm in here!"

My eyes were still half-closed. I barely looked her way and headed to the toilet. "I just have to pee fast. I won't flush," I said, taking myself out of my boxers over the bowl.

"You can't pee next to me!" She said nastily.

I smirked and turned my head towards the shower. "You wanted me to pee on you, but I can't pee next to

176

you?" I asked sarcastically. The shower door flung open, and her head poked out crossly.

"We said we would never talk about that again!" She quipped.

Now looking through the steamed glass shower door, I noticed a design on her hip. It was hard to see the blurry image through the fogged glass. Tucking myself back in my boxer briefs, I approached the shower.

"You got a tattoo?" I asked, going in for a better look. She pulled her head back inside the shower and tried to shut the door as I held it open. "Let me see."

"No, get out of here!" She said, trying to hide her body. I watched the water soak her as she wrapped her chest with one hand, and her other covered between her legs.

"Oh, stop being a baby; I've seen you naked a million times. Let me see the tattoo," I said, now unbelievably interested.

"I wouldn't say a million times," she argued, still trying to hide.

"You don't know how many times I watched that tape," I said. "C'mon, let me see it."

Slowly she turned her body to display her hip. Orange and yellow flames were inked on the side of her body. It started from the side of her butt and trailed up her hip, and rested right under her rib cage. I gazed riveted. "That's hot," I commented.

"Thank you," she said. "Now get out."

"Okay, okay," I said, laughing, and flushed the toilet before running out.

I heard her squeal in the bathroom, then rushed out with a towel around her. "You dick!" she said, now grabbing a pillow from the bed and attacking me with it. I covered my face in a defensive position as she kept hitting me with it.

I started towards her, arms extended to grab the pillow from her.

"What is this – a pillow fight? What do you think? I am one of your girlfriends, and we're at a slumber party?" I asked, getting close enough to grab the pillow from her. I threw it off to the side as she continued to slap me with her hands.

"Is everything porn in your head? That's not what girls do at parties," she said.

"Stop hitting me!" I warned. She kept swatting at me until I backed her up towards the bed, and she fell backward on it. I got on top of her and grabbed both her wrists in one hand. As I held them down above her head, I asked:

"Do you need to be restrained?"

I was now on top of her, with my body positioned between her legs. I could feel her wet towel against my bare chest. Staring intensely into each other's eyes, as if my lips were a magnet drawing to hers, unexpectedly, we were leaning into each other. Just as my top lip grazed hers, I heard Heather call in. "Guys, you awake?"

I stumbled as I quickly jumped back off the bed, as Heather and Pete came in from their run. Amber pushed herself up into a sitting position, holding up her towel tight to her chest.

"The water looks amazing. You guys want to go for a swim?" Pete asked. I looked uneasily from Pete to Heather, who seemed clueless to what had almost just happened. I wouldn't even glance in Amber's direction.

"Let me change into a bathing suit," I said, rifling

through the dresser drawer.

It was only eleven a.m., but the beach was already packed with lounge chairs. Umbrellas were practically on top of each other, and the sun was glistening off the water, making it an even brighter teal blue. The water was so clear you could see the fish swimming in the ocean—a big difference from New York City beaches. Even the sand was more of a white color than the usual beige we had grown accustomed to. When we got out of the water and wanted drinks, the service was somewhat slow due to the enormous crowd. When I suggested I'd go to get drinks from the bar, Amber offered to help. We didn't say much to each other as we headed over to the bar.

The bar wasn't as packed as the beach, so there were stools we could sit on. I sat down on one, enjoying the shaded area much more than the sand. I looked over at Amber and noticed her shoulders were already getting red from the sun. The bartender passed the Bloody Mary I just ordered, then turned around to make the other drinks.

I took a sip and must have winced.

"What's wrong?" Amber asked.

"Try that," I said, sliding the drink to her. She took a sip.

"It's missing something," she said, licking her lips and squinting her eyes.

"I know; it's bland," I agreed. She thought about it for a second.

"Horseradish?" She asked.

I nodded. "That's it! The horseradish – you should go behind the bar and show them how to make a real Bloody Mary," I teased.

"You make them better than me," she said, as the

bartender now handed her the rum runner she ordered. That was the nicest we had been to each other in months.

I shook my head as she sipped her drink.

"No way, you make them better," I argued.

Smiling at me, she turned her body on her stool towards me and reached for my hair. She held a lock between her fingers and commented, "Your hair is curling."

"I know you liked my hair curly, so I dunked my head in the ocean for you," I said flirtatiously. She let out a giggle and took her hand off my hair. I pushed my hair back and attempted to fix it.

"That's the most romantic thing a man has ever done for me," she said. Running my hands from my lap to my knees, I leaned into her and said: "I hope not."

There we were, somehow locked in each other's gaze again. The bartender slid Heather and Pete's drinks in front of us as we stayed paralyzed in each other's stare. "Your shoulders are getting burnt," I said, breaking the silence. She lifted her shoulder to look, when from behind me I heard, "Hello sweetheart!"

I felt my mother's hands around my shoulders as she kissed my head. I turned my body around to face her.

"Hi, Mom," I said as I kissed her on the cheek. "When did you get in?"

My mother was always decked out no matter what the occasion. She wore a very flattering long yellow sundress with classy jewelry, paired with oversized round sunglasses and heels. She was in very good shape, and her long wavy dark hair and olive complexion made her look ten years younger than she was. She looked like she had just arrived from Hollywood. Amber stared at my mother, speechless.

"My God, James wasn't kidding; you are stunning!" She uttered out, almost uncontrollably. My mother turned to me in amazement.

"You called me stunning?"

I smiled awkwardly. "No. I mean, yes, I said you were beautiful, but Amber had asked me where I got my eyes from. So it's not as creepy as it sounds. This is Amber, by the way."

Amber extended her hand to shake my mother's. "It's so nice to meet you, Mrs. Nisan!"

"Nice to meet you as well, Amber. Yes, James did get his eyes from me, but I will have to credit his father for most of his good looks. Such a handsome man he was," she replied. Amber smiled. "What are you guys up to?" She continued.

"Well, Amber is a bartender also. We were just talking about who makes a better Bloody Mary," I said, holding up my drink. "Would you like a drink, Mom?"

"Oh no, thank you, but a Bloody Mary-making competition sounds like fun," she said, smiling approvingly at Amber. She leaned into Amber and added: "It's nice that you bartend also. Take it from someone who was married to one, it's hard to run on their schedule." Realizing my mother must have thought Amber and I were a couple, we both pulled away from each other simultaneously, laughing.

"Oh, no, no, we're not together," I said.

"No, I work for him," Amber added. My mother stood there confused.

"You aren't together?" She repeated, now shooting me a skeptical look.

"No, this is Pete's girlfriend," I said. "I'm here with

um..." I started looking over my mother and passed the dining area to the beach to get a glimpse of where Heather could be. "I'm here with Heather. I'm not sure where she went. We were on the beach just before. Pretty, tall, blonde, lingerie model...." As I was rambling out words, Pete came up behind my mother.

"Hey, Mrs. Nisan! You look beautiful as always!" He kissed her on the cheek.

"Hello, Pete," she greeted him.

"I see you met my girlfriend," he said, putting his arm around Amber. "I was wondering where you two went off to."

"Here – sit," I said, jumping up and offering my mother the stool. She just stood looking at me, disappointed.

"I'd rather not," she said in a dismissive tone.

Picking up on her tone, Pete grabbed Amber and said they'd see me back at the beach. My mother sat in Amber's seat and ordered a mimosa. "What are you doing?" She asked me, not looking at me.

"What do you mean?" Trying to change the subject, I followed it up with, "When did you get in?" The bartender brought over her mimosa. She took a sip then turned around to face me.

"Pete's girlfriend? I was watching the two of you for five minutes before I came over. I saw the way you were looking at her," she said.

"Looking at her? How was I looking at her?" I asked, taking a sip of my drink.

"Like your father used to look at me," she answered. Just as I opened my mouth to say something, Heather came flying over to me, wrapping her arms around my waist.

"I was wondering where you disappeared to!" she loudly exclaimed. I could immediately smell the vodka on her breath. No doubt my mother could as well, judging by the dirty look she gave her.

"This is Heather," I said. "This is my mother."

My mother looked Heather up and down, unimpressed. "Hello, Mrs..." she stopped dead in her tracks and looked at me. "I just realized I don't even know your last name. What's your last name?" She asked me. Talk about timing. Just when I thought things couldn't get any worse, Heather shows up at the completely wrong moment.

"Nisan," I said, almost under my breath.

"Hello Mrs. Nisan, it's so nice to meet you," she said and then hugged my mother. I almost spit my drink out of my mouth as I watched my mother pull back from being soaked by Heather's wet bathing suit against her clothes.

"I'm so sorry," Heather exclaimed regretfully. She started wiping my mother's dress with her hands as if her palms were some sort of sponge.

"I'm fine, really," my mother said, annoyed. Embarrassed, Heather said she was going to find Amber and Pete and departed after apologizing again. Getting right back to her drink, my mother was silent. I sat there uncomfortably, waiting for her to say something.

"Lingerie model, huh?" She finally managed to get out. I just nodded. "James, what happened to you? You grew up with a man who adored his wife. He was an amazing husband and father, and yet you chose to idolize your brother. Why?"

I just looked down. I didn't really know the answer to that. I didn't have one. She was right, and my father was all of that. I didn't know why I wanted to be like Rob so much growing up, but I did. "Your brother is finally getting married," she continued. "How are you going to have kids without a wife?"

I held up my pointer finger. "Oh, it's simple, I'm...." She held her hand up to stop me from saying anything else.

"I don't want to hear your idea of how you think you are going to have children without a wife. You are going to be thirty-six next month; when are you going to grow up already?"

I took another sip of my drink without looking up. Talk about a buzz kill. I didn't have an answer for that either.

Chapter Twenty-One

During the rehearsal dinner, I could feel my mother stare at me the entire time. She was analyzing my interactions with Heather, examining me from afar. I could tell she liked Amber and thought she was a better fit for me. Comparing me to my father earlier wasn't fair. Thinking of him when I was growing up, watching him adore my mother the way he did. I remembered thinking back then that I couldn't even fathom what it felt like to be that much in love with someone. She thought growing up with a man like that should have made me be like that. Instead, it was the opposite. He created this impression in my head that I felt I could never live up to. I just wasn't like him, plain and simple. Not many men were. I guess that's why my mother was so in love with him.

For most of the dinner, I found myself distracted,

wondering what Pete and Amber were doing. Were they out having a good time in south beach, or worse, were they in the room alone, having a good time with each other? When we were finished with dinner, I took Heather out to a club. The last place I wanted to go was to the room. We stayed out dancing all night and got back to the hotel around four a.m. Quietly sneaking past the pull-out couch on the way to the bedroom, I spotted Pete's arm around Amber as she slept. Looking down at them, I regretted requesting the bed and having to walk past them to get to the bedroom.

The wedding was quite the event. The affair must have cost my brother a quarter of a million dollars. The venue was incredibly classy, and he had to have had at least three hundred guests. Decorated only in silver and gold, all the tables were holding white roses and mini champagne bottles as gifts for the guests. The wedding gift table took up the entire wall, and I questioned silently if the gifts were empty decoys as decorations, considering the number of envelopes in the box. The bride, Brianna, was a beautiful magazine cover model. Tall with wavy long blonde hair, green eyes, and a six-pack. Everything a magazine model should be, and unlike Heather, she was all-natural. They made a good-looking couple. I could tell Heather was intimidated by her, so I had to keep my distance from them.

After the bride and groom danced, the DJ called all the couples onto the dance floor. I danced slowly with Heather, which just felt bizarre because she was in heels again and taller than me. I kept glancing over at Pete and Amber dancing. Her head on his chest, his arms around her waist. When the song was over, I walked out on the balcony to smoke a cigarette. I needed air. I found myself avoiding people for most of the wedding: Brianna and Rob, Amber and Pete, my mother.

It had stopped raining, and the weather was perfect as I leaned over the ledge of the balcony, looking off at the palm trees. There was a slight breeze, so I wasn't too hot in my tuxedo jacket, and it made the trees sway nicely. My mind was now fixated on the waving trees. With basically everyone I knew in that one room, I somehow never felt more alone. I was snapped back into reality when I heard the balcony door open. I glanced over my shoulder, and Amber was walking towards me. She was wearing a long, tight backless black gown with a slit up to her thigh, showing just a hint of her fresh tattoo. Her hair curled the way I like it; she couldn't look more beautiful. She was wearing high stilettos, which I could tell were making her uncomfortable while dancing; she was walking a little funny. She dug through her purse and took out a cigarette.

"I think we are the only smokers in Miami," she said, lighting it.

I approached her, going inside the breast pocket of my tuxedo jacket, and took out a pack of cigarettes to show her.

"I always find it funny, at every wedding; towards the end of the night, everyone is smoking – even the nonsmokers. I always bring another pack as a backup," I answered.

She inched closer to me. "I take it you forgive me?" She asked. I turned back towards the ledge of the balcony, looking away from her and leaning on my elbows. I took a pull of my cigarette.

"What gives you that impression?" I asked, exhaling

the smoke. She leaned up against the ledge right next to me, so close that her arm was grazing mine.

"I mean, you did try to kiss me in the room," she said, taking a pull of her cigarette. I turned my body around to face her, still leaning on the ledge.

"I only tried to kiss you because you gave me a face," I justified. She turned her body now to face me also.

"What face?" She asked.

I bit my bottom lip and squinted my eyes, imitating the face that suggested she wanted me to kiss her. Her mouth dropped as if she were offended.

"I did not! You gave me that face!" She insisted, making the same face I had just made.

I straightened myself up and crept closer to her. "What face did I give you?"

She made a face again. Before I knew it, I dropped my cigarette, pulled her into me, and began kissing her passionately. She clutched me by the back of my neck and pulled me into her lips harder. Without taking my lips off of her, I backed her up against the wall. I guided her around to the side of the venue, where no one could see us. Placing my knees between her legs and pushing them open, I was now rested between her legs, rubbing my body on her. The kiss got more intense as the seconds progressed, her hand sliding down my chest, undoing my tuxedo jacket. Her hand wandered down my chest to my stomach, then back up. I held her by the neck into me; my other hand was running up and down her bare back.

"We shouldn't do this," she muttered, not taking her lips off mine.

"You're right; it's really bad," I concurred, pulling her even closer to me.

Her hands now traveled up my chest and around my neck as she tugged my hair, guiding my lips down to her neck. My mouth had no choice but to follow her lead.

"You're my best friend's girlfriend," I uttered into her ear. Then the sentence I just said occurred to me as if it were the first time I heard the words out loud. I pulled back from her and repeated it, now holding my forehead in revelation. "You're my best friend's girlfriend."

I buttoned my tuxedo jacket and looked up to the sky, realizing now exactly what I had done. I hooked her up with my best friend. I started fixing the back of my hair as she ran her fingers through hers, repairing it as well. We composed ourselves and walked back around to the balcony as if nothing had happened. I lit another cigarette.

"James, I'm so sorry I looked at your videotapes," she said. I took a pull of my cigarette and looked at her.

"Yes, to answer your earlier question, I forgive you. I probably would have done the same thing had I come across a bunch of videos of you with other dudes," I confessed. "Does he make you happy?"

She looked directly into my eyes and nodded. "Yes, he does."

"Good. Friends?" I asked, now accepting it was over. There was nothing between Amber and me anymore. She had a boyfriend now, who was my best friend. It was my fault, but it was the reality of the situation. I needed to move on.

"Friends," she conceded. I heard the balcony door open once again, and now Andrew came out.

"Am I interrupting something?" He asked, looking from Amber to me. We both shook our heads no. "You have an extra cigarette?"

I took the pack out of my pocket and handed him one. "And so it begins," I said, looking at Amber.

"I'll see you inside," she said as she turned to leave me alone with Andrew. I held out my lighter and lit his cigarette.

"I have a funny story for you," he said, once we were alone.

"Oh yeah, what's that?" I asked, putting my lighter back in my pocket.

"So, I am at the bar ordering this beautiful gin martini," he said, holding up the martini glass, displaying it for me as if it were a work of art. "And Pete is behind me. He introduces me to his girlfriend, Amber," he said, motioning to where Amber had just been standing. I put my cigarette out and wrapped my arms around my chest, leaning back on the ledge. "She looked so familiar. I knew I had seen her somewhere before," he continued.

I studied the expression on his face, not exactly sure where he was going with the story. So, he carried on. "Pete told her I owned the steakhouse on Second avenue – she said she had never been there before. Then Pete says to me: 'Amber works for James, maybe you have seen her at the bar'. And that's where I remembered where I'd seen her. She *was* at the steakhouse; only she was there with you!"

I dropped my arms and straightened up from the ledge.

"Did you say this was a funny story?" I asked.

"Well yeah, not like laugh out loud funny – more like ironic funny," he answered. "How long were you fucking her for?"

I started biting on my thumbnail. "Six months."

"Does Pete know?"

"No."

"Six months! Damn James, I've known you for what twenty-five, twenty-six years? I have never seen you with the same girl for more than a weekend. Do you remember what you told me that night when I asked who she was?"

I looked past him. "No, what did I tell you?"

"You said she was the mother of your children," he said.

I looked back up and held my hand up. "That was a joke – we had just been talking about if we were both single when I am forty...."

"Come here," he said, cutting me off, and facing the glass door, looking through to the dance floor. He pointed at Amber and Pete dancing. "What do you see?"

I studied them dancing, Pete twirling Amber around, and her laughing. "I see two of my best friends having a good time," I answered. He nodded.

"Okay, think of this. And you don't have to answer me, but I want you to think about it for yourself. Is that an image you can watch for the rest of your life? We're not kids anymore, James. People don't date for fun. The next wedding we're attending could quite possibly be theirs. Hey, you'll probably be the best man for that one. Looking forward to hearing that speech." I didn't say anything. He put his cigarette out. "I don't know what you did, James, but you better fix it." And with that, he walked back into the wedding.

The night ended pretty late. They were all shot, but I was wide awake. I walked a few blocks up to the liquor store and bought a bottle of Jameson. Back at that hotel, I put on a bathing suit and quietly grabbed a glass, and went to sit out on the balcony. I planned to go in the hot tub, but I sat at the table and slowly sipped my drink first. A few minutes later, the door opened, and Amber emerged. I looked up at her, my lips still to the glass. Placing the drink on the table, I looked at my watch.

"It's only two a.m. These regular people don't get that at two a.m. we are just getting the night started," I commented.

"Where'd you get the Jameson?" She asked.

"There is a liquor store on Collins Avenue. Grab a glass."

She went inside and came back out with a glass. I poured her a drink and she sat down at the table and took a sip. She looked around, taking in the scene.

"God, I love these palm trees. So different than New York," she said. I looked up where she was looking. The sky was blue and purple, the stars so bright—no skyscrapers, no smog; just palm trees for miles, flapping in the breeze.

"Yeah, it is beautiful," I agreed.

"Why are you wearing a bathing suit?" She asked, noticing my attire.

"I was going to go in the hot tub. You want to go in?" I asked. She said okay, then went back into the room to change into a bathing suit. When she came back out, we took our drinks and headed to the tub. Her new tattoo looked incredible with the red bikini she was sporting— her curled hair up now, in a messy ponytail. I could feel her stare at me as I took off my t-shirt. I got in first, and she followed, sitting across from me.

"I can't believe Rob got married. Assholes like us don't get married," I said, still in disbelief that I had just attended Rob's wedding.

"You're not an asshole," she said.

"Sure I am – just look in your phone. The biggest one, if memory serves me correctly." She let out a laugh.

I took a sip of my drink, then set it down and laid my head back, staring at the stars. "You know when I was in the army, we would take turns sleeping, Jim and me. I would stare at the stars to keep myself awake. It's funny, no matter where you go, that one star – that really bright one, is always there," I said, pointing up to show her which one I was referring to. She looked at me, surprised I was talking about the army. It shocked me as well; I never spoke about it. Then she moved in next to me to get a view of the star.

"That's not a star. That's a planet," she said.

"Really?" I asked, not sure if she was kidding or not. She smiled.

"Yes, it's Venus. It got its name because of how bright it is. It's named after Venus, the Roman Goddess of beauty, love, and victory." I took a sip of my drink, listening to her speak. She cleared her throat, embarrassed. "I'm kind of an astrology geek. And a nerd when it comes to Roman mythology."

"Why 'victory'?" I asked.

"She was in love with Mars, the God of war. It was said she would lead him into battle, and when she did, he would come out victorious," she explained. I took another sip of my drink.

"So that's the whole Mars, Venus thing? They were a couple?" I asked. She looked down at her knees, raised just above the water.

"No. She was married to his brother, Vulcan. The God of fire."

"Did they ever end up together?" I asked.

"No," she replied. I took a deep breath.

"That's sad. You know, you're way too smart to be a bartender. You're wasting your talent," I said. She didn't respond. "You know, when you think of all these stars – or planets – whatever – how long they've been around. Everything they've seen, you ever think, what's above them? Who or what calls the shots? Who decides who gets to go home and who doesn't?"

She shifted her whole body to face me, her facial expression getting serious. "James, what are you saying?"

I wasn't truly sure what I was saying. I had never spoken about this to anyone before. I wouldn't even discuss it when they made me go to therapy. I had no control over what was coming out of my mouth. "He had a wife, a son – why'd I come home, and he didn't?"

"Look, if you're implying it should have been you...."

"No, I'm not saying that or implying anything. It's just; I had no one here who needed me. Sure, I guess a few people would have missed me, but it wouldn't have impacted anyone's lives had I not come back," I explained.

"I didn't know you then, but it would have impacted my life had I never met you. Meeting you helped me with so much," she said.

"I impacted your life?" I asked, letting out a chuckle. "How did I affect your life at all? Helping you get over Evan?" I took a sip of my drink at his name.

"I mean, yes, there's that. But there's more than that. You gave me a job. You ended up becoming a good friend, and you're not an asshole. You don't lie to girls; you keep it real at all times. You don't pretend you're something you're not."

"Do you think I am a narcissist?" I asked, remembering the conversation I had with Paul in Vegas.

"A narcissist? No, you're not a narcissist. You have this invisible wall up around you, always. One day though, you're going to meet a girl that satisfies you so much, you won't have the desire to be with anyone else. You're going to want to go to sleep with her every night and wake up with her every morning," she began. "And you know what? When you meet that girl, the wall will come down, and she is going to be lucky."

I wanted to kiss her so bad. In retrospect, that should have been the night I told her. Told her the truth. That she was the girl that satisfied me so much that I hadn't slept with anyone else when we were sleeping together, but I didn't. We had agreed earlier that we were just friends.

Chapter Twenty-Two

I had feared Miami so much initially, but it probably was just what I needed for some closure in the end. Mine and Amber's working relationship had gotten much better now that we agreed to be friends. We went right back to the way we were before it all happened – before she became my 'significant nobody'. Heather and I never hooked up again, and it didn't get weird going to the gym. We were cordial and even still flirted, although neither one of us ever had any intentions of doing anything physical again.

A month had gone by, and Pete and I went to Atlantic City for my birthday. I was playing blackjack when I spotted him from the corner of my eye, motioning me to go over to him. I finished my hand, took my chips from the table, and walked over to him. "I'm on a roll. What's going on?" I asked.

He put his hand on my shoulder and leaned into me. "Bro, I just hit the jackpot. Well, *we* did. Look over there," he said, pointing to a set of slot machines. Two pretty girls in their mid-twenties sat there playing machines, both dressed to go out for the night. "They invited us to go to the club with them. Dibs on the brunette," he said, smiling.

I studied the girls, who were laughing with each other. As if they sensed us looking at them, they both turned around and smiled in my direction, and the blonde one waved at me. I half waved back and now looked at Pete.

"Dibs on the brunette? What about Amber?" I asked. He squinted his eyes and gave me a look of confusion.

"What about Amber? She's not here," he answered. I backed up and looked back over at the girls, and let out a deep breath.

"Come on, man. You told me you weren't going to hurt her. You gave me your word."

"How am I hurting her? How will she even find out? Are you going to tell her?" He asked. I wrapped my arms around my chest and looked up towards the ceiling.

"Well, are you?" He asked again, annoyed.

All I could hear was the ringing of slot machines beating through my head. How could he ask me a question like that?

"No, I am not going to tell her, but what is the sense of having a girlfriend if you're still going to fuck around with other girls?" I asked, feeling my temper itching to come out.

"These girls are here from Alabama and looking to have a good time. It's a once-in-a-lifetime opportunity, and it's not like I'm out looking for girls. It just happened. Stop being so cynical, and no one is even saying anything sexual is going to happen. Let's just go out with them, have a good time. Go with the flow, it's your birthday!" He argued. Reluctantly, I followed him over to meet the girls.

Kay, the brunette Pete called dibs on, stood to shake my hand. She was tall and thin with short brown hair and blue eyes, with her left arm sleeved out with tattoos of a floral design. She was wearing a fire red dress and black pumps. "Heard it's your birthday; Happy Birthday," she greeted. I nodded as a silent thank you, and then the blonde, Felicity, stood.

"Are we going out?" She asked, looking me up and down. She was wearing a black mini skirt and an olive-green crop top that matched identically to her eyes. She was tiny, had to be five foot three with heels on. She had this cute southern twang that gave her a sort of innocent yet sexy vibe. I couldn't help but smile. She was so cute.

"Has any man ever said no to you?" I asked, staring into her green eyes.

"Not yet," she said, biting her bottom lip. "Are you going to be my first?"

"Not for that," I answered, and the four of us headed to a club.

As the hours progressed, I was glad I went out with them. I was having a great time with Felicity. She was so full of energy, and I couldn't get enough of her accent. I kept asking her to say certain words and couldn't help but get a kick out of how she pronounced them. Dancing until we were slick in sweat, we made our way to the bar for another round. She was so different than the girls I was used to, a soft-spoken, sweet country girl – the complete opposite of New York girls. I was so into her, that I hadn't been paying much attention to Pete and Kay, who were off on the dance floor doing their own thing.

"How long are you here for?" I yelled over the music, handing her another drink.

"Only Sunday," she said, moving her face to my ear so I could hear her. The guy next to me got up from his seat, so I sat back into it and pulled her against my lap. She slid her shoes off and held them in her hand.

"My feet are killing me!"

"You are so small!" I said, standing for a second to measure her height to my body as I gently pulled her head to my chest.

"Are you making fun of me?" She asked, pouting as if I hurt her feelings.

"No," I said, shaking my head slowly, slumping back into my seat. "I love it." I pulled her closer to me and gradually leaned into her, planting my lips on hers. "You taste good too," I commented, licking my lips and tasting the remnants of cherry lip gloss she left behind.

She bowed into my neck, her hand on my thigh, and said, "I was sent to you from the universe as a birthday gift."

I smiled. "Looks like the universe knows me very well. It is just what I wanted!" I joked. She ran her hand from my thigh to my crotch. Instantly getting stimulated by her touch, I straightened up on the stool and repositioned myself.

"From the feel of things, you are going to tear me apart," she said as if she were daring me. I bent close into her ear and said, "I'll be gentle, I promise."

Before long, we were in the elevator heading up to my room. The elevator was crowded and, of course, it just had to stop on every floor. Felicity had her back to me, brushing up and down on me in the corner. It was hard to control myself from picking her up against the wall and having my way with her. I didn't even care how many people were in that elevator; she had me so turned on.

When we got to my room, I turned the light on and immediately pulled her down to my lap on the couch without hesitation. Rubbing herself against me and kissing my neck, I pulled off her shirt. I ran my hands over her breasts, to her neck, and then grabbed a bunch of her hair and pulled her tighter into me. Her lips pressed firmly against mine; I could taste the vodka on her breath. She pulled my shirt over my head and unbuttoned my jeans. She hovered over my lap just enough for me to slide my pants down and put a condom on.

She let out a moan as I slipped myself in her. Still clutching her by the hair, I pulled her aggressively into me. The rougher I got, the more turned on she became. I was so into it, so into her. Then out of nowhere, she picked up her phone and scrolled for a number. I was stunned at first when she put the phone on speaker. It was Kay, who was also now in Pete's room next to mine. The two girls started talking dirty to each other while Pete and I continued with them. They were describing what each of us was doing to them in graphic detail. It was like they were having phone sex with each other, and Pete and I were somehow just their sex toys. That was new territory. Listening to both girls moan in excitement got me even more aroused. I almost lost control of myself before Felicity stopped me. That's how turned on I was. She climbed off me and said:

"Save it for Kay."

I sat there speechless, unsure what she even meant by that as she left the room, until Kay walked in and joined me.

She crawled across the floor to me and perched herself on my lap, backward. Through the speaker of her phone, I could hear that Felicity had now got to Pete's room. It took about ten minutes before Pete and I both got off, and Kay pushed herself off me. She hung up the phone and kissed me. "You guys were fun. Happy birthday," she whispered in my ear, then got up to leave. I laid my head back on the couch, panting. I felt paralyzed and in a daze; my head was spinning. I couldn't believe that had just happened. So much for sweet and innocent.

A few minutes later, there was a knock on my door. I slid up my boxer briefs, and Pete came in, boasting. "Bro, what the fuck was that?" He exclaimed, now sitting on the couch next to me. I could still barely breathe, still trying to process what had just occurred.

"Did that really just happen?" I asked, turning my head to him. He started laughing.

"It sure did. Did I tell you we hit the jackpot or what? Just like old times," he said, grinning ear to ear. I put my forehead in my hand and rubbed my temples. Yeah, just like old times, except he had a girlfriend now. And that girlfriend was Amber. In a crazy way, I felt like I was the one who cheated on her.

I never mentioned to Amber what happened that night in Atlantic City. How could I? I certainly wasn't going to be the guy who told her that her boyfriend cheated on her. Her boyfriend, my best friend that I had somehow unintentionally set her up with. Annoyed one night, she looked up at me as I made a drink and said,

"Does every guy cheat?" I passed the glass to the customer and tried to pretend I didn't hear her. Guilt came rushing over me, my heart raced, and my palms grew wet with sweat. When I finally made eye contact with her, she stared at me wide-eyed, waiting for an answer.

"What? No, I mean, I don't know – why?" I asked, trying to play it off. I was waiting for her to tell me how she found out that Pete had cheated on her. I wondered how much she knew and anticipated what I could have told her as a response.

"Those brokers over there," she said, pointing to the table in the corner, shaking her head in disdain. "I just dropped off their drinks, and one is 'training' the other on how to cheat right—telling him about some crazy chick who made a fake social media page about him and how he had to pay her off. With all of that, he has the nerve to try and explain to him why he *can't* leave his wife. I mean, look at them, James, they have to be in their forties. When does it end?" I looked over to the men she was speaking about. She was right. They were probably in their mid-forties, both very well-dressed stockbrokers in good shape. I raised my eyebrows.

"If your man were that rich, maybe you'd think differently," I said.

"How do you know how much money they have?" She asked as she started making another round of drinks. "You make a lot of money, and I wouldn't know it by looking at you."

"What's that mean? I look like I'm broke?" I questioned.

"No, but you don't look rich," she said.

"Because I'm not rich, I don't make *that* type of money. I can see the diamonds on that guy's Rolex from here," I said. She finished preparing her drinks and brought them over to another table. When she returned, she was right back on the same subject.

"I wouldn't care how much money my man had, I would still leave him if he cheated on me," she said firmly. I didn't say anything. All I could do was wish she never found out about Pete, and if she did – she absolutely could not know I was involved.

By the time Christmas had rolled around, I finally let mine and Pete's Atlantic City encounter leave my mind. I had realized that both Amber and Pete were grown adults, and Amber wasn't my problem. As far as I knew, that was the only time Pete had cheated on her, so I just decided to mind my own business. However, the second I walked into my mother's house, she asked: "Where's Pete?"

I kissed her on the cheek and walked past her. After placing the wrapped gifts I had been carrying under the tree, I took my jacket off and hung it in the closet. "Nice to see you too! He's not coming," I simply replied.

"Why?" She asked, a look of concern on her face. "He's here every year for Christmas. Are you guys fighting?"

I followed the scent of spices into the kitchen, where there were trays of food on the counter. My mom's house had been the same since I was a kid. It always smelled of something fresh she was cooking or baking, and sometimes, especially around the holidays, a mixture of pine from the tree. She is the only person I knew who still had carpet in the house, and even though I typically wouldn't say I liked the look of the carpet, it gave me a very welcoming, nostalgic feeling. I could imagine what it felt like on my bare feet as Rob and I would chase each other around the house when we were little. I still had a rugburn scar on my knee from a wrestling incident between us.

"Rob helped you put the tree up?" I asked as I grabbed one of the lamb meatballs with the toothpick from the tray. I was usually the one she called for help with the tree. She slapped my hand.

"Stop picking, save your appetite. There's a lot of food," she scolded me.

"Oh, stop, it's an appetizer; it's supposed to be eaten first!" I heard the rumbling of footsteps upstairs and looked up.

"Yes, Rob helped with the tree. I didn't want to bother you, and they are staying here. He and Brianna are upstairs getting ready. Why didn't Pete come?" She asked again.

"Pete has a girlfriend now," I said, swallowing the meatball and throwing the toothpick in the garbage.

"And what about you? When are you going to get a girlfriend?" She asked.

I rolled my eyes and headed towards the living room as she followed behind. "You know," she continued. "One day, this is going to stick out," she touched my stomach, "and this is going to recede," now touching my hairline, "and you'll need a good girl who is going to want you for more than just your looks."

I ran my fingers through my hair as I sat on the couch and grabbed the remote to turn on the TV. "I'll worry about it then; right now, it's all still here," I said, tugging a little on it. She sat down next to me on the couch.

"What are Pete and Amber doing that they couldn't come here?" She asked.

"I don't know. I didn't ask," I replied, as my attention was now on the TV, searching for a channel to settle on.

"Did you not ask him because he has a girlfriend or because of who his girlfriend is?"

I put the remote down and faced her. "Mom, I don't have a thing for Amber!"

No sooner did the words leave my lips, Rob came flying down the stairs. "You have a thing for Amber?" he asked. I threw my head into my hand dramatically.

"No, I do not have a thing for Amber!" I said, getting louder and annoyed.

"Good," he said as he plopped into the armchair across from me. "If she's anything like her friend Mia, stay away. That girl makes my skin crawl!" He shook his body as if we were cringing. "Nasty, cocky little bitch. I really can't stand her," he continued his rant, clenching his jaw.

"I don't think she likes you much either," I said.

"Really? What gives you that impression?" He said, almost amused by my comment.

"Why don't you just fire her if you hate her so much?" I asked.

He stood up to get a beer from the fridge. When he returned, he threw one in my direction as he opened his. "She happens to be a great bartender and draws in a crowd. I'm lucky I live in Miami; I could never work here with her." He sat back down as he sipped his beer.

"Yeah, like you'd be 'working' even if you lived here," I joked.

Rob hadn't bartended in years. As soon as he earned enough money to open the second spot in Miami, he hired an entire staff at both places. He hadn't 'worked' in years.

"Speaking of, I wanted to talk to you about your bar. I stopped by the other day."

I popped open my beer and looked up at him, waiting

for his criticism. "Go ahead; what's wrong with my bar?"

"How much does that bar bring in?" He asked.

"I take home about half a million a year," I answered.

My mother looked back and forth from me to Rob. "You can be doing three times that in that area. Rip out the high tops, put in some couches. Up the clientele. I have celebrities who come into my place, and they are buying bottles at a time." Rob was always more of a businessman than me, always so focused on making money. Half a million dollars wouldn't cut it for him.

"I am perfectly happy with my clientele, thank you. What is this, get on James day?" I asked, looking back and forth between him and my mother. "Where's Brianna? Brianna!" I beckoned. "Come save me, please!"

Brianna came down the stairs. "What's wrong?" She asked as she leaned down to kiss me hello, and then sat to the other side of me on the couch.

"Apparently everything. I don't make enough money, I don't have a girlfriend...."

"Oh, I have someone perfect for you," she interjected. I held my hand up.

"Stop, stop – I. Like. My. Life!" I said slowly. "How was the honeymoon?"

She smiled and ran her fingers through her hair. She knew I was intentionally trying to change the subject, but she played along. "It was incredible! Bora Bora, this time of year is fantastic; I just wish it was longer."

"You get knocked up?" I asked.

My mother slapped me again. "James!"

"What? It's a valid question!"

Brianna shot Rob a dirty look and walked into the kitchen. He licked his teeth as he watched her walk away, then threw his gaze back at me. "Bad subject to bring up, man. She's mad I don't want kids."

"You don't want kids?" I exclaimed in shock. "Then what is the point of getting married?"

"Good question," he responded, lifting his beer can towards me as a silent cheer.

"Oh, I don't know; how about *love*?" My mother chimed in. Brianna reappeared in the doorway.

"The table is set. Come, let's eat," she stated coldly.

The four of us gathered around the table with an uncomfortable silence in the air. Holidays didn't seem the same anymore since my father died. A seat was always left empty for him at the table, out of respect. There was just something missing, especially when he used to say Grace before we ate. My mother had Rob and I alternate throughout the years, and I was thankful this was his year. The feel of Christmas was completely different now. No one ever addressed it, though, and it was as if we were all just playing along and going with the flow.

I found myself wondering a lot during dinner why Rob didn't want kids. Did Brianna know that before they got married? That seemed to be a big thing to disagree over as a couple. Would he change his mind? Would she really give up the idea of having children if that is what she truly wanted?

Chapter Twenty-Three

The holidays came and passed, and now it was January and getting a little busy at the bar when Pete called on Friday night.

"You're not going to believe this. They are here!" He started the conversation with. I moved my phone to the other ear and held my finger to the other to hear better. It was so loud with the jukebox playing in the background and the crowd laughing and drinking.

"What? Who's here? Where?" I asked.

"The girls from Atlantic City – Kay and Felicity. They are in New York this weekend, and they want to hang out with us tonight. Good thing that one of us takes phone numbers!" He exclaimed. I looked over at Amber, who was busy in conversation with one of the customers.

"I can't; I'm working," I said.

"You own the bar, call in another bartender and come meet me," he proposed. Amber turned around and caught eye contact with me as if she could feel my eyes on her. She threw me a grin.

"No, I'm too busy," I reiterated, getting lost in her smile.

I hung up and went over to help a customer. He called right back, and I sent him to voicemail and put my phone on silent.

Amber was in an abnormally good mood that night as I tried my hardest to act casual. She was so happy, smiling, joking, bubbly, I was not going to do anything to jeopardize her energy. I loved seeing her this way. But it wasn't me, or even Pete, who ruined her mood that night. It was the call she got at almost eleven when she gasped, and it seemed as if I watched the glass she was holding fall in slow motion before shattering to the floor. She had one hand over her mouth in shock, the other holding her stomach as tears started streaming from her eyes. She looked like she was about to collapse. Kaitlyn rushed over to sweep up the glass, and I ran over to her and grabbed her by the waist.

"What's wrong? Are you okay?"

She looked up at me, tears gushing down her face. She could barely speak.

"I have to go," she said, hysterical. "It's my mom. I have to go."

I told Kaitlyn to call in a backup bartender and grabbed Amber by the hand. I pulled her through the crowd of people and led her outside, immediately hailing a cab. She was in no mental condition to go there by herself. It was as if I was holding her body in place, her knees seemed like they were going to give out at any moment.

When we arrived at the hospital, I immediately knew the doctor's look as he approached Amber and what was about to come out of his mouth. I'd seen that exact expression on many people throughout the years. He was bearing the burden of being the one to tell a family member that their loved one had just died. My mind went blank. I didn't even hear what the doctor said. I just held Amber's head into me as her body warped into my chest.

We didn't say anything in the cab on the way to her apartment. It was when we made it inside that she broke the silence.

"I've been calling and texting Pete, but I can't get him," she said, sinking into the kitchen chair. I studied the placemat on the table.

"You should eat something," I said. "I'm going to go to the pizza place on the corner and get us some food. I'll try to call him also," I said and walked out of the apartment before she could ask any questions. I walked up to the corner and dialed Pete. He immediately picked up.

"Where are you? I called you three times. These girls are too much to handle on my own," he said. I could hear Felicity in the background, urging me to come meet them.

"I'm at Amber's place. Pete, her mom died," I said. There was a pause.

"Is she there with you now?" He asked nervously.

"No, I went to the pizzeria to get food. She's been trying to call you."

"I know, but it's midnight. Normally I'd be sleeping at this time anyway. So don't tell her you got through to me," he answered. I stood there, stunned with anger.

"Pete, did you hear what I said? Her mom died," I

repeated. Again, another silence. "Pete?"

"Yeah, I am here. Look, she doesn't know that I am aware of that. She'll be dead tomorrow too."

I could feel the blood bubbling throughout my veins. I wanted to reach through the phone and choke him to death. I always knew he could be a dick, but now he'd gone too far. It's one thing to be a cheat. It's another to be completely insensitive and so selfish that he couldn't comfort his own girlfriend. Trying to keep calm, I said:

"You better shut your phone off, and we never had this conversation."

With that, I hung up on him and also shut my phone off.

I walked into the pizzeria and ordered two chicken cutlet parmigiana heroes. My head was in a cloud. I was trying to comprehend what had just happened with Pete—thinking of what I was possibly going to say to Amber when I got back upstairs. "Will that be all?" the cashier asked.

I looked down at the glass counter in front of me, trying to bide time. I randomly pointed at different plates of food displayed. "No, I'll have some rice balls, zucchini sticks... what is that? Garlic knots? Give me an order of that. Throw some beef patties in. Maybe the stromboli, that looks good; give me that too. Oh, an order of baked ziti...." Before I knew it, I was walking out with two bags of food.

When I arrived back in Amber's apartment, she was still sitting at the table. Her head rested in her palms, her eyes puffy from crying. I went over to the counter and started unpacking the bag and making her a plate of food. She looked over at the containers on the counter.

"What the hell did you get? Are you sure you're Greek and not Italian?" she asked, trying to make a joke. I placed a plate of food in front of her and sat down. I nodded.

"Yeah, I'm pretty sure. You can freeze it; you'll have it for the week," I said, forcing a fake smile.

"Did you get in touch with Pete?" She asked, pushing the food around with her fork but not eating it. I shook my head.

"No. Maybe he's sleeping," I lied.

She looked down at her food but still didn't take a bite. "Yeah, maybe he's sleeping," she repeated. "I'm sorry, James, but I'm not hungry. I need to go lie down."

"Okay," I said and got up to start wrapping up the food as she went into the bedroom. After I packed it back up and put it in the freezer, I washed the dishes and then went into the bedroom. She was lying down, still in her clothes as I stood over her bed.

"I cleaned up the kitchen for you. The food is in the freezer if you get hungry. Is there anything else you need? Are you going to be okay if I leave?" I asked. She didn't answer, not that I was really expecting one. I sat down on the bed next to her. "If you think of anything you may need, just call me."

She placed her hand on my thigh. "Will you stay with me? Until we can get ahold of Pete?"

I placed my hand on top of hers, looking into her big brown eyes. "Sure," I said faintly, knowing full well we wouldn't be getting in touch with Pete.

I laid down next to her, staring up at the ceiling as she nestled her head on my chest. Instinctively I started running my fingers softly up and down her back as I continued staring up, trying to keep myself calm. I wasn't, though; I was anything but calm. My blood was boiling; I was so mad at Pete. I knew exactly where he was and who he was with. I knew what they looked like, smelled like, and tasted like – both of them combined wasn't half of Amber. I felt like my body was trembling with rage. My only saving grace, the one thing that was keeping me at ease, was the scent of strawberries from Amber's shampoo pouring into my nostrils. Her soft hair on my chest was somehow the equivalent tranquility of taking a sedative.

"James, will you do something for me and promise you won't ask any questions?" Amber asked, breaking me out of my trance. I looked down at her, her middle finger slowly tracing my chest, where she knew my dog tag tattoo was under my shirt. I had no idea what she would ask me to do, but there wasn't much that I would say no to.

"Yes," I said, wishing she were going to ask me to murder Pete.

"Say the words. Tell me you promise," she repeated.

"I promise," I whispered, looking directly into her eyes.

Unexpectedly I felt her lips on mine, and her smooth tongue entered my mouth. I had never kissed a girl that felt like it did when I kissed her. Her kiss penetrated through my entire body. She was the only girl in my lifetime that I could have kissed all night long and been satisfied without doing anything else. She pulled away from me a little, and with her top lip still against mine, she said quietly,

"Don't say anything, just pretend you love me tonight."

My tongue instantly sank into her mouth, and I rolled over, now facing her. We caressed each other's bodies until we were tenderly stripping off each other's clothes. We laid there for a while, kissing and stroking each other's bodies.

I rolled her over and got on top of her, my tongue grazing her neck lightly. I felt her hands run up and down my back as she intertwined her fingers in mine. Suddenly, the vision of every woman I had sex with flashed before my eyes. The realization hit me, that sex had been an antidote for me to mask my own sorrow, to subdue the grief. It occurred to me this was exactly how I was coping with my own loss—random and meaningless sex. I couldn't let her go down the same rabbit hole; I wouldn't let her do it. I removed my fingers from hers and pushed myself up over her, looking down at her. "I'm sorry, I can't do this," I said softly, rolling off her. She turned her body to face me, an astonished look on her face, her hand still on my chest.

"Are you turning me down?" She asked. Truth be told, it was the hardest thing I ever did. I wanted her so bad, but at that moment, I just couldn't.

"Not like this," I began. "This isn't you. You are with Pete, and you're the furthest thing from a cheat. I cannot be the person you wake up regretting being with."

She let out a small laugh and rolled her eyes in complete disbelief.

My fingers caressed her back as I continued. "Love and sex are two very different things. If I did love you, I wouldn't be sleeping with you right now."

"Oh no?" she asked. "What would you be doing?"

I pulled her into me and held her tightly. "I would let you know I am here for you; make you see that you're not alone. I would hold you in my arms all night, hoping to somehow help ease your pain."

I ran my fingers through her hair as she steadily rubbed my chest. We remained silent for a while before we were simultaneously gawking into one another's eyes. The tears started pouring down her cheeks again as I kissed them off and held her closer to me. I was gripping her so tightly I was afraid my embrace would crack her ribcage. I felt her bare foot brush against my calf as she wrapped her leg around me.

That was the most intimate thing I had ever experienced, despite it not being sexual. It was at that exact moment when I realized just how insanely in love with her I was. I hadn't moved on, and there was no moving on. I wanted to tell her. I wanted to let her know how much I loved her. I needed her to understand how I wanted to take care of her, always. But she told me not to say anything. She knew. It just didn't matter – it was too late. She was already with Pete; I lost my chance. I was just the rebound guy, the significant *nobody*.

When I woke up the following morning, her body was still wrapped in mine. I kept my eyes closed and pulled her in tighter. I knew the minute I opened my eyes; it was over. That could quite possibly be the last time I ever woke up next to her again. Her phone rang and forced both our eyes to open. She held the phone up. *Pete.* She didn't pick it up right away. She stayed locked in my embrace a little longer. Then she sat up and picked it up.

"Hey, babe," she said. "Yeah, I figured you were sleeping." *Sleeping? Please, he's a piece of shit that doesn't deserve you;* I felt like screaming. "Okay, yes, thank you so much. See you soon."

She hung up and looked down at me. "He got my message; he took off work today. He'll be here soon with breakfast," she said. I sat up, scanning the room for my clothes.

"Okay," I said, retrieving my clothes from the floor. She looked down at the ground as I got dressed. She couldn't look at me. Humiliation all over her face as if she immediately regretted trying to sleep with me the night before. I turned to leave when she stood. "James, wait," she said.

I turned around and started back towards her as she reached into me and hugged me.

"Thank you for being there for me," she said.

I hugged her back, intoxicated once again by the scent of strawberries.

"No problem. Take as much time off as you need. Don't worry about the money, I am going to pay you," I assured her.

I went straight to my apartment and stood in the shower for forty minutes. I found myself once again trying desperately to wash off the scent of her. Ferociously scrubbing my body, I felt like daisies and strawberries were seeping from my pores. I rested my hand on the tile wall, almost holding myself in place and letting the water stream off my body.

Grief is a funny thing. You think you're fine, and then it just hits you out of nowhere. All I could picture was Jim. Watching him die and remembering sitting the next day in depression, knowing that his wife Tanya would know exactly why the officers were at the door before they could even tell her. I had imagined her sitting down with their two-year-old son, telling him that he would never see his dad again. My hands started shaking as I steadied my grip on the shower wall. My heart was pounding, my breathing becoming heavy. Guilt overwhelmed me for not grieving for my father the way I should have. Visions tormenting me of what I had become; insensitive, numb, inhumane.

A few years after Jim died, I recalled Tanya kissing me also, trying to convince me that Jim would want me to be with her and watch over their son. I had agreed with her that he would want me to look after Christopher, but sleeping with his wife, I was sure, was definitely not something he would have chosen. It had been years since I had an anxiety attack of this magnitude.

I got out of the shower, dressed, and went into the medicine cabinet, digging through all the prescription bottles to find the anti-anxiety medication they had prescribed when they forced me to go to therapy after returning home. Most likely expired by now; I wondered if they actually went bad or just lost effectiveness. I took twice the dose just in case, went into the living room, and stared at the fish tank until they kicked in.

Chapter Twenty-Four

Another month had passed since that night with Amber in her apartment. She had taken two weeks off, and aside from the funeral, I hadn't seen her at all. All I could think about was the encounter we had during that time – how it was so unlike anything I had ever experienced with another woman. We never spoke about it, but I had become obsessed with feeling that again —some sort of connection with someone outside of lust. I must have slept with a dozen types of women that month. Black, White, Spanish, Asian. Redhead, blonde, rainbow-colored – yes, really, she had rainbow hair – purple, pink, and blue. Not one had come remotely even close to that night with Amber.

It was now February, and an entire year had passed since that night we had rebound sex for the first time. The night that turned my whole life upside down. I was perfectly fine with my life before that had happened. I should never have slept with her. I would have been none the wiser.

"Uncle James..." Christopher said, annoyed. I must have accidentally been ignoring him. I looked over at him across the table. It was Thursday night, and we were having dinner. "Are you going to eat that?" He asked, motioning at the plate in front of me. His tone implied it wasn't the first time he asked me. I looked down at the ziti in front of me and slid it over to him.

"No, I'm done."

"You still thinking about that chick?" He asked.

"No," I lied.

He put his elbow on the table and leaned his face in his hand, slanting his head and raising his eyebrows in disbelief. "Okay, yes," I admitted.

"What do you like so much about her?" He asked.

"I don't know. She's not like other girls."

"How?"

"She's just... I don't know. Like what's the complete opposite of conceited?" I asked, racking my brain for the right word.

"Modest?" He suggested.

"No, not that. Oblivious. Completely, almost comically oblivious to how hot she actually is. She's smart, thoughtful...."

"Why don't you just tell her how you feel already?" He asked, shoveling a forkful of ziti in his mouth.

"It's not that easy."

"Why not?" He asked. "Are you afraid?"

"No, I'm not afraid," I said defensively. "It's just not that simple."

"Sounds simple to me," he said, now washing his food down with soda. "What do you have to lose?"

"For starters, my best friend," I began.

He rolled his eyes. "Your 'best friend' is a dick," he said. He was right about that. "Plus, why would she even tell him? If she did, then she'd have to admit that she never told him she slept with you in the first place." The second good point he made.

"When you were like four, I took you camping; you remember that?" I asked.

"Yeah," he said, looking very interested now. He loved when I told him stories of him as a kid. It didn't matter how old Christopher ever got; he would always ask me to "tell him a story."

"You were begging me to have a kid. You kept saying you wanted a cousin. I told you I wasn't ready to have a kid; you know what it's like trying to explain to a four-year-old why you want to be single?" I laughed at the memory. "Now, twelve years later, I feel like I am still explaining my relationship status to you."

He put his fork down and took another sip of his soda.

"You need to be in a relationship to have a 'status'." he said.

"Whatever happened to 'it's complicated'? Is that not a thing anymore?"

"But why is it so complicated? You're so into this girl. So, you lose your dick of a 'best friend', big deal. What else is holding you back?"

"Okay, fine – even if you're right about that, I still have to work with her," I explained.

"So, you think it's a better working relationship if you just had pointless sex with her and didn't have feelings for her? I'm confused," he said sarcastically. I reached my fork into his plate and took some pasta. Looking at this sixteen-year-old boy, making more sense than anyone else in my life. He was always far beyond his years.

"I think I tell you too much," I said, in between chewing. He grabbed my phone. "What are you doing?"

"What's your password?" He asked. I reached over to grab my phone from him.

"Give me back my phone," I said.

He pulled the phone back and laughed, finding this all very amusing. Then, he started typing numbers into my phone, and it opened.

"How do you know my password?" I asked, annoyed.

"I set your phone up for you, remember?" He said, grinning and scrolling through my phone. I thought he was just messing around with me, pretending to type something, when he slid the phone back to me. I looked down.

"Holy shit, you actually texted her... you little asshole," I said, aggravated. The message read: *Hey, can you come in a little earlier tomorrow? I wanna talk to you about something.* "How do I un-send this?"

He took another forkful of food and shrugged. "You can't."

I looked down at the phone in a panic, trying to figure out how to take back the text message when it vibrated in my hand.

What time? She replied. I rested my forehead on my hand. Without lifting my head, my eyes shifted up at Christopher, who was now eagerly studying me, curious to see what I was going to write.

I sighed and shook my head. *Four p.m.,* I wrote.

Okay.

"You happy with yourself?" I asked Christopher, throwing my hands up in the air. He smiled playfully.

"Yes, actually, I am. When the two of you get married, I better be the best man," he said.

"Yeah, well, if the two of us do get married, I'll be out a best friend, so I won't have many other options," I teased back.

"I'll make sure to include that in my speech," he said.

The next day, I showed up at the bar at four p.m. Nervously pacing back and forth, I took a shot of Jameson to take the edge off. Practicing over and over in my head what I was going to even say to her. She came in and set her bag down. Bruce was still in his shift, so I pointed at the door leading to the yard. She nodded, grabbed a cigarette, and followed me out. As I lit my cigarette, trying to put my thoughts into words, she began.

"I need to talk to you about something too."

She needed to talk to me about something; that was a good sign. Did she feel the same way and was going to make this easier on me? "You go first," I said, taking a pull of my cigarette. I anxiously waited to hear what she was going to say, hoping she would confess she was in love with me also.

"Next weekend is Valentine's Day, and Pete wants to take me to the Poconos. Can I have the weekend off?" she asked, exhaling her smoke. That completely threw me off my game.

"No," I abruptly answered. She was taken back by my bluntness.

"No? Why not? Bruce has been dying for hours, and he will gladly fill in for me."

"I'm going away with someone," I made up quickly.

"You're going away with someone for Valentine's Day?" She asked, undoubtedly not buying a word I was saying. "Who?"

"None of your business," I scoffed.

"You're lying! You just don't want me to go away with Pete! You're jealous!"

"Jealous?" I snickered. "I'm not jealous. I don't give a shit about you and Pete. I just happen to be going away. With a girl. A girl you don't know about. I don't tell you everything that happens in my life."

"You're a cock block!" She exclaimed.

She took a pull of her cigarette and stepped closer to me, clenching her jaw.

"I don't believe you. You just don't want Pete and me...."

I cut her off. "Believe me, I am. And about you and Pete, I could really care less. It was just sex. You meant nothing to me. You were just a good fuck." I'm not sure if it were the words I said or the tone I said it in, but her bottom lip trembled a little as she shifted her gaze down, dropping her cigarette on the floor.

I could see the tears forming in her eyes as she stared at me like if she could stab me dead right there, she would. "I'm going home. Find someone else to do my shift, prick," she said irately and stormed out.

"Fine, go home," I yelled. I stayed outside and finished my cigarette before I walked back into the bar. Kaitlyn wouldn't even look up as she was preparing for her shift. I could only imagine what Amber told them as she left.

Bruce approached me. "Do you really want me to cover Amber's shift?" he asked.

"Yes," I said crossly. "And call your brother, see if he wants to work tonight; I'm also leaving." I went back to my apartment and drank alone until I passed out.

The next day I was still aggravated while I was at the gym. As I was spotting Pete, he said he wanted to talk to me about something.

"Go ahead," I said coldly.

"I'd rather not do it when you're holding two hundred pounds of steel over me," he said.

I put the barbell down and straightened my stance. "What's up?" I asked.

"It's about Amber," he said. I turned my back to him and held my hand up.

"I'm not talking to you about Amber," I said. I started walking away from him.

"She told me what happened between you guys," he said, his voice raised louder so he could assure I heard him. I turned back around to face him, stretching my neck from side to side.

"Look, Pete, don't involve yourself, okay?"

"Don't involve myself?" He repeated. "She's my girlfriend, James. And you...."

I rolled my eyes. "Oh please, stop. I will tell you the same thing I told her. I don't care that you're her boyfriend; I'm not jealous. It doesn't even phase me. It was sex Pete, that was it. Just fucking sex!"

He let out a gasp and glared at me, stunned. "You had sex with Amber?"

My heart sank into my stomach. Evidently, that was not where he was going with that sentence before I interrupted, I realized.

"I'm sorry, I must have misunderstood. What were you

going to say?" I asked, letting out a nervous laugh.

"Back up," he said, now in a challenging tone. "You slept with Amber?"

I looked down. I didn't know what to say.

"Did you sleep with Amber?" He repeated, this time anger filling his voice.

"Before you," I reasoned.

"How long before me?"

"I don't know," I answered.

"You don't know? How long were you sleeping with her?" His voice was now getting louder than before.

"I don't know," I said again.

"Then fucking guess," he said, now yelling.

"Six months, give or take."

His face turned red. He started rocking his body and cracking his knuckles as if he were getting ready to punch me in the face. I hadn't seen him this angry since we were teenagers.

"So, you gave me your leftovers?" He hollered and shoved me. I tumbled back a bit but caught myself before falling.

"No, if we're being honest, I wasn't done with her!" I said, raising my voice to his level and pushing him back. A crowd began forming around us. People were leaving their machines to see what the commotion was.

He gritted his teeth, shaking his head and waving his finger towards me. "So, you're both liars. I asked her numerous times if she slept with you. *You,* specifically! Did you sleep with *James,* and her answer was always no!"

I held up my hands. "Okay, in her defense, we agreed not to tell anyone."

"Oh, you agreed?" He asked sarcastically. "So, her

loyalty should be to you and not to me?" *Loyalty*. That was it; that was the trigger word. The only person I should have cared about being loyal to this whole time was Amber.

"And what did you do? You fucking cheated on her!"

As if someone had just removed a pin from a grenade, I was now enraged. I shoved him so hard he fell back into the weight bench. Stumbling, he got up and swung to punch me in the face, but I caught his arm midair. I held him down by his head, holding his arm behind his back in a position that I could have broken with one jolt. It took three guys to break it up. Two of them just to pull me off of him, and one to hold him back. He kept trying to break out of the hold and lunge towards me, now out of breath.

"The two of you can have each other. I'm done with her, and I am done with you!" He hissed. I grabbed my towel and went to the locker room to get my things.

Chapter Twenty-Five

Once I walked out of the gym, I heard his voice from behind.

"We're not done," he said.

"Really? Wasn't that just your parting speech? That you were done with her and me?"

He swung his fist and landed straight on my mouth. Now, I usually would have easily escaped that blow, but something in me needed to feel it. Something within me craved for him to punch me. I lost it in that instance, and a scene broke out in the middle of the street. Blow for blow, hitting each other. Anyone watching would not have guessed we were best friends at one point. He got that one free punch in, but before I knew it, he was right back in the hold I had him in a few minutes prior, except this time I lost control. I couldn't help myself, and I broke his arm with one swift nudge.

The next thing I knew, I was face down on the ground, a knee in my back and my arms being pulled together behind me. I felt the steel against my wrists as the cuffs clicked tightly. The cop helped pull me up to my feet as he led me towards the direction of the cop car. As he tilted my head down to put me in the back, I watched Pete be put into the ambulance. Talk about a dramatic exit.

I'd become a pro in the army of estimating the amount of time that had passed without having a watch. Since they confiscated all my possessions, including my shoelaces, I had guessed it was roughly twenty-three hours that I was locked up. I watched them bring Pete in a few hours after me, sporting a cast on his arm. He's lucky that is all I broke.

"Nisan!" I heard my name called as the cell bars slid open, "You made bail, follow me."

I followed the police officer, who looked ten years younger than me, through the hallway. He was a bit shorter than me but stocky. At least he looked it in his NYPD uniform, walking with authority. I always found it fascinating how different these men looked in regular clothes. I walked past the criminals handcuffed to the benches and police officers filling out paperwork. I could feel the stares on me as some jerkoff yelled out, "pretty boy," in my direction. The cop turned to me briefly before we made it to the door and looked up at me. He shifted his eyes for a second, then looked back at me.

"Thank you for your service," he said, a little above a whisper as if he'd get in trouble for saying that to me. As he handed me a box of my belongings, I let out a breath.

"Yeah, you too, I guess," I muttered, practically ripping

the box out of his hands. I walked into the waiting room to see my mother sitting on the bench waiting for me. She stood up when she saw me appear and looked me up and down with worry all over her face.

"Are you okay?" she asked.

"I'm starving," I simply replied. She nodded, and we walked a few blocks to a diner in silence. Once seated, I could smell the fresh coffee and steaming eggs and realized I was even hungrier than I thought. I hadn't had anything in twenty-four hours, and my stomach was rumbling. She ordered breakfast, but I ordered a burger with fries and handed back the menu to the waitress. As soon as she walked away, my mother finally spoke.

"We need to talk," she said softly.

"I already know what you are going to say," I replied, not looking up, playing with the paper placemat showing off advertisements of local businesses in the area.

"Do you? What am I going to say?"

"How disappointed you are in me," I guessed, still refusing to meet her eyes.

"Look at me," she said, in a more welcoming than demanding tone. I looked up and made eye contact with her. "I briefly spoke to Pete before you came out. I am sure you know Amber bailed him out."

"I assumed," I said, now folding my hands on the table.

"So, I have an idea of what happened. No, I am not disappointed in you. I'm relieved," she stated.

"Relieved?" Definitely not where I thought she'd be going with the conversation. She crossed her legs and leaned onto the table to get as close to me as she could.

"I know you don't like to talk about your past. What you've been through, what you've seen – what you've done. And you don't have to. But I know you're tormented by many different emotions; grief, guilt, sadness. You question your self-worth...."

"So, what you're saying is that I'm broken," I interrupted her.

"Maybe, but a lot of things break; it doesn't mean they can't be fixed. I am relieved to see that despite all these terrible feelings you may have, you can still love." The waitress came over and dropped our food off.

"What's the point? Even if I did love Amber, it's just more heartache," I said, taking a bite of my burger. I winced, forgetting I had a fat lip until that bite.

"You'd be surprised at what love can heal," she continued. "Everyone has a past, maybe not as traumatic as yours, but things that scar them. It's what makes us who we are. The events in someone's life aren't what defines them. It's how they handle those events, that make them who they are. The choices they make, how they move on, why they keep going. You breathe, you bleed, you *feel* – you're human. You can try to hide your emotions behind this 'playboy' exterior, but who you are inside will find a way of showing itself. I know therapy wasn't for you, but you cannot hide that you are human, no matter how hard you try."

I swallowed my bite and took a sip of my soda. "Please don't suggest a dog; I don't have the lifestyle to have a dog," I said. She let out a laugh.

"I'm not suggesting a dog. I'm suggesting you recognize and accept what you're experiencing. Stop hiding behind bimbos and alcohol. You have a lot to offer someone; there is more to you than what you show. I'm not saying this because I am your mother. I'm saying this because I know you, and you're a lot more like your father than you like to admit."

I rested my head in my hands. "I do miss him, you know. I realize I didn't handle his death the way I should have," I admitted.

"I know you do. You handled it as you needed to at the time. Everyone grieves differently."

"Mom, I know you like Amber, but that's just not going to happen," I said, lifting my head and going back to my burger.

"Maybe it won't. Maybe it's not supposed to. Maybe she isn't the one. Maybe she was brought into your life just to show you that you're capable of loving someone. There's a lot of 'maybes' here. No one has the answers. That's what life is – a bunch of maybes. The question you need to ask yourself is, is she worth fighting for? And I don't mean physically, even though your instincts must have told you that – you fucking broke Pete's arm!" My eyes shot open in shock that my mother had dropped an F-bomb.

"He deserved it," I said.

"I don't know all the details, but for you to do that to your best friend, I am guessing you're right that he did."

Putting my burger down, I stood up and went over to her side of the table. She slid over to let me in. I put my arms around her shoulders and pulled her into me, hugging her tightly. She ran her fingers through my hair like she used to when I was a kid, my head resting on her shoulder. I stood back up and went over to my side of the table.

"I love you, James, and I am incredibly proud of the

man you are becoming, even if I had to bail you out of jail," she said.

I let out a laugh. "Thanks, I love you too."

Chapter Twenty-Six

I sat on my living room couch that night, fixated on the fish on the coffee table. I was watching them swim around so carefree, ignorant, oblivious to the life around them. My cellphone was lying on top of it. I had been waiting for two hours already, expecting it to vibrate. Amber was going to flip out, and it was already four p.m. No way she would wait until we started work to rip me apart. All I could think about was what was possibly going on between Pete and Amber at that moment. He was going to break up with her. Was she crying? Was she yelling? Was she somehow relieved because, deep down, she was really in love with me?

I felt the underarms on my t-shirt dampen with sweat as I massaged my temples with my thumbs, anticipating the phone to go off at any second. Instead, I nearly jumped out of my skin when there was a loud knock on my door. I sat there for a few seconds, hesitant to move before the pounding got louder. Grudgingly, I stood and made my way to the front door and casually pulled it open.

Amber stood in front of me, bearing a facial expression I had never seen on her before. Her cheeks were flushed, and her eyes glistened with tears. "Where is she?" she screamed in rage, pushing past me, exploring the rooms of my house, on a mission. Then, after checking all the rooms, she flew back to me while I was still speechless in the living room. She shouted again, "Where is she?"

"Where is who?" I calmly asked, having no idea what she was talking about or who she was referring to.

"Your slut of the day, where is she? I am going to ruin your relationship just like you sabotaged mine!"

Frozen, I just looked down. It was hard to look at her like that. She was furious, hurt, gawking at me as if I betrayed her.

"There's nobody here," I said.

She stormed into the entertainment room as I followed her. "Amber, can we please talk?" I asked desperately. She picked up my iPad from the dresser and threw it at me.

"Delete it," she demanded. "Delete the video of us."

Holding the iPad, I smirked. "Trust me; I deleted that a long time ago. You know, right after you snuck out of my house that night."

Her face got even redder. "Not that one, the first one!"

I sat on the bed, still holding the iPad. "That was such a good video," I reasoned.

"Delete it!" She repeated, tears now falling from her eyes. My heart raced even faster; it was killing me that she was so upset. I patted the bed next to me.

"Why don't you come to sit here and talk to me?" I pleaded. "Maybe we can watch it. We had so much fun that night. Remember, I asked you to make a sexy face – and you made a constipated one? We were having such a good time, back when we enjoyed being around each other?"

"Watch it? What are you, insane?" She asked and didn't budge. "How could you tell Pete about us? We promised we weren't going to tell anybody! The second I am finally happy you need to go and kill it. You claimed you're not jealous? You broke his fucking arm! What kind of animal are you?" I didn't answer; I just looked down. She was probably right. I was an animal. "Why did you do that? I finally found a good, decent boyfriend, and then you had to go and destroy...."

"He cheated on you!" I blurted out, now getting angry also. She took a step back and stood there motionless. She was shaking her head in disbelief.

"No – bullshit, you're lying," she said, now lowering her voice.

"I'm not. He cheated on you. I was there," I said calmly.

"When?"

I took a deep breath and exhaled. Then, I looked directly at her, and I said, "In Atlantic City, on my birthday," I replied.

"In Atlantic City? What did you guys' tag-team someone yet again?" she asked, her voice growing louder.

"Not exactly," I began. "I was with someone, and he was with her friend. They weren't from around here, Alabama, I think – somewhere down south. I don't remember exactly where. At some point, in the middle of having sex with this girl, she called the other one on the phone. They switched rooms, and well – I guess you could say we swapped." She stood there speechless for a second.

"So, he slept with two girls? Are you fucking serious right now? What kind of men are the two of you? Is this real fucking life? You swapped?" She fired out questions, disgusted.

"Yes. And then one night they were in New York, and he met back up with them again," I continued.

"Oh, *he* met up with them again," she let out a laugh and rolled her eyes. "Only him? And where were you?"

I started moving the iPad around in my hand, feeling the edges. I was nervously turning it around and studying it as if I'd never seen an iPad before. I couldn't say it. I couldn't get the words out.

"Where were you?" She repeated the question.

I placed the iPad on the bed and stood up to approach her. There was no easy way to say this. "I was with you. It was the night your mother died." She backed up away from me, a look of horror on her face, as she went over to the bed and slowly sat on it.

"Amber," I said softly, trying to move toward her as she held her hand up to stop me from coming any closer. "Can we just talk, please?"

"So, you did get ahold of him that night? And you lied to me. I should have known better than to date anyone affiliated with you!"

My regret instantly turned to anger. Once again, she was throwing all the blame on me.

"You know what? I am so tired of you blaming me for everything like you're some sort of fucking angel. You like to pretend you're this 'good girl'; what makes you so much different than me? You went from Evan, to me, to Pete. You think because they were your boyfriend or fiancé or rebound sex; whatever label you want to give them, you're any different? You're not! You're just a hoe on the low." She stared at me in silence.

"Why didn't you tell me? And please don't give me that 'bro code' bullshit."

"I didn't want to hurt you," I answered honestly.

"Well, you hurt me more by not telling me than you would have if you did. But then again, I meant nothing to you, right? Just a good fuck?" she threw in my face.

"Amber, I was mad. Maybe you're right, perhaps even jealous; I didn't mean...." She picked the iPad up from my bed and handed it to me.

"Delete it," she commanded, not wanting to hear anything else I had to say.

I opened the tablet and went to the video. I displayed the screen to her as I pressed the trash can icon.

"Permanently delete it," she said. I rolled my eyes and went into the recycle bin and permanently deleted it.

"There, it's gone – are you happy now?" I asked.

"Yes," she said, nodding. "I hate you. I never want you to see my face or any part of my body again."

I sat back down on the bed and let out a laugh. "That's gonna be hard since we work together."

"I quit."

I chuckled at first but then got serious when I saw the stern expression on her face. "What? Are you serious?" I asked.

"Yes, I'm serious, I quit – and don't try to call me," she said, as she picked up her phone and made me watch her, as she scrolled down to *Biggest Asshole* and blocked my phone number. "Have a great fucking life," she concluded and marched out of my apartment.

I honestly thought that she would calm down. I truly believed she just needed a few days, and she would come to her senses and realize this was ridiculous. I basically did her a favor, telling Pete. He was a dick, and she deserved better than that. I broke the guy's arm for her. I proved my allegiance was to her and not him. But an entire week had gone by, and I hadn't heard from her. By the following Friday at the bar, when Kaitlyn and I were closing up, she approached me.

"You need to hire someone," she said.

I didn't look at her. Instead, I kept my eyes focused on the money I was counting.

"I know," I said, nodding.

"She's not coming back," she softly reiterated, as if she were afraid of what my reaction was going to be.

"I know," I said again.

"She got another job," Kaitlyn elaborated. I put the money down and looked over at her. She really wasn't coming back. She got another job.

"Where?" I asked.

"The new club on First," she answered. The club she was referring to had opened a month earlier and was all everyone spoke about recently. It was the hottest new club in the area and was packed every night.

"That's a good place," I said. She nodded in acknowledgment, still waiting for my answer on hiring a replacement. Finally, I put my hand on her shoulder and looked her in the eyes. "Congratulations, you're now the manager. Hire someone."

"Really?" she asked excitedly.

"Yes, really," I said and went back to counting money. "You're a good worker, and I trust your decision."

It took her two days to hire Amber's replacement. Max, a good-looking guy in his early twenties, started that next weekend.

Chapter Twenty-Seven

The following month dragged by. One month felt like a year. It was like I was in some movie, where every day you wake up, nothing changes, and everything about the day is the same as the last. All I did was work and go to the gym. A different gym, I now had to join because of Pete. I couldn't stop thinking about Amber. It occurred to me I would have instead had her dating my best friend, or fight with her, then not have her in my life at all. I was so used to seeing her face every time I walked into that bar for the last six years, that it felt like a piece of me was missing. I hadn't hooked up with another girl. I didn't even flirt anymore. I was over it, over all of it. I was over women.

Max was working out well at the bar and drew in a younger female crowd. He was energetic and funny and probably what the bar had needed for a long time.

Thursdays became just as busy as Fridays and Saturdays, so I started working with them on Thursdays also, after my weekly dinner with Christopher, of course.

Max, Kaitlyn, and I were working on Saturday night when I heard a female voice call me from behind.

"Can I have a dirty martini, please? Extra dirty." I turned around to see Isabel sitting on the stool across from me. I made her the martini and slipped the glass over to her. "Do you like things dirty, James?" She asked flirtatiously.

My eyes wandered from hers down to her cleavage protruding out of her tiny shirt. Then, finally, back up to her eyes. The one girl Amber never wanted me to sleep with – and here she was, in front of me, inviting me with her eyes. If Satan could send up a temptress himself, it would be Isabel.

"I do," I said.

"Can I have a cherry?" She asked. I put a cherry on a napkin and handed it to her. She held the cherry in her hand and sensually put it in her mouth, sucking on it and then biting down on the stem and pulling it off. "It's been a while since I had a cherry."

I leaned up on the bar, leaning my chin on the palm of my hands. I always had a thing for Isabel. She was unbelievably sexy; her presence alone turned me on. Amber wasn't even speaking to me anymore; all rules were off now, right? She smiled.

"Where's Amber?" She asked.

"She doesn't work here anymore," I said harshly and straightened myself back up. She rested her chin in her hand and leaned towards me.

"I guess it's been a while since I've seen her," she said.

Wrapping my arms around my chest, I leaned back on the bar. So, she didn't speak to Amber; therefore, Amber wouldn't find out. But, you know what, who cares if Amber found out? I decided. She slept with my best friend; she can't say anything anymore.

"Did you come here to see Amber or me?" I asked, winking at her.

She pulled her bottom lip into her mouth with her teeth. "Always you," she said. "You know, I've always wondered – what are the ingredients to a 'sex on the beach'?"

"Vodka, cranberry juice, orange juice, and peach schnapps," I answered, gazing intensely into her eyes. She took a sip of her martini.

"And what are the ingredients to sex in your bed?"

Making it blatantly clear to her that I was looking her up and down, I replied, "A sexy Spanish brunette with a great rack and a gorgeous set of blue eyes." She looked down, pretending to be shy, then looked back up at me.

"Want to show me how to make it?" She asked. I looked down at my watch. It was only two a.m. My attention turned to Max and Kaitlyn, who immediately tried to pretend like they were working and not listening to our conversation.

"You guys okay closing up?" I asked. They both nodded, and I left with Isabel.

"I need a second to freshen up," she said as we walked into my apartment. I went into the entertainment room as she went into the bathroom. I sat on the bed, patiently waiting for her to join me. She strolled in and came right over to me, sitting on my lap facing me. She leaned in, and her lips pressed up against mine as she slipped her tongue in my mouth. I started taking off her shirt. Her eyes drifted past me as they examined the room.

"Where's the camera?" She whispered into my ear. I should have figured she knew about that. All these girls talk. I pulled her up and rolled her over on her back, sliding off my shirt. Her hands ran up my stomach to my chest.

"No cameras," I said, pulling off her skirt.

She sat up promptly. "What? I put on extra make-up, get the camera," she said, disappointed.

"I'm not in the mood to videotape," I said, simply, now running my fingers around her panty line. I shifted them over and started licking her as she pushed my head away, annoyed. I looked up at her as she held me by the hair.

"I'm not hot enough for you to videotape?" She asked, insulted.

"Fine," I said, getting up and setting up the iPad. That made her smile. She instantly started getting erotic for the film, sexually posing and making erogenous sounds. Obviously not a beginner to the world of homemade porn. I went back over to the bed as she grabbed my pants by the waist and pulled me into her, unbuttoning my jeans while her mouth unzipped them. She was getting aggressive, taking down my pants, putting me in her mouth, and moaning, saying dirty things. Then something occurred that had never happened to me before. I lost it. My erection was gone; I looked down, just as surprised as she was.

"It happens to a lot...." She began when I cut her off.

"No, it doesn't. Not to me," I quipped. Now she was working extra hard to get me stiff again, and I was freaking out. All I could think of was: this is Amber. She was somehow magically cock blocking me like she had some sort of sixth sense and knew what I was doing. Suddenly everywhere I looked, I saw Amber. Sitting on the loveseat, lying on the bed. I could hear her voice telling me, *"There are literally hundreds of girls in New York City that would be more than willing to sleep with you; why do you have to go after my friends?"*

"Let's go in the living room," I suggested, praying the vision of Amber would stay in bed where I left her. She followed me into the living room as I sat down, and she started dancing on my lap. Being a stripper, it didn't take her long before she got me aroused again; she knew what she was doing to perfection – she was a pro. She continued with the dirty talking and exaggerated moans even though the iPad wasn't rolling anymore. Finally, I turned her over on the couch and thrust inside of her, her groans now getting even more extravagant. I reached over and put my hand over her mouth to soften her cries, and she bit into my hand.

"You want it rough?" I asked, still with my hand over her mouth. She pushed herself back into me, hard, implying she did. The act didn't take more than fifteen minutes. When we were through, she went back into the entertainment room to get her clothes and dressed as I sat down on the couch. She came back in, leaned over, and kissed me.

"That was long overdue," she commented. I looked up at her as she was fixing her hair.

"Can you not tell Amber about this?" I asked. She looked at me, puzzled.

"Why not? You have something going on with Amber?"

"No," I said. "We didn't leave on the best of terms, you

know, at the bar. I don't need her knowing my life." She looked at me suspiciously but agreed. As she left, I stayed sitting on the couch staring at the fish, once again feeling like I cheated on a girl I wasn't even in a relationship with.

A few weeks had passed since I had hooked up with Isabel, when Max was trying to get into the safe while we were closing on Thursday night.

"Hey James, what's the password to the safe?" He asked.

"It's Amber's birthday, um...." I thought for a minute. "7 9 8 5." So much for taking my mind off of her.

I watched him plug the numbers in as he repeated them out loud. "7 9 8 5. She's thirty? Damn, she looks a lot younger than thirty," he remarked.

"You know her?" I asked, now concentrating on clearing out the empty bottles and not looking at him.

"I met her a few weeks ago. She came in here," he said. I stopped and looked back at him in shock.

"She came in here? To this bar? When?"

"I don't know, a few weeks ago," Max answered.

"For what?"

"A drink. She ordered a flaming marshmallow. Then, after watching me make it, she asked for a Kettle One and soda. Said she hated making that and wanted to put someone else through hell making it," he said, shaking his head. Of course, she did. She really hated making that drink.

"Did she say anything about me?" I asked, trying my hardest to sound nonchalant.

"Kaitlyn did most of the talking to her. I just made her a drink," he answered. My focus now turned to Kaitlyn, who looked like she was afraid to answer the question.

"Did she say anything about me?" I asked again, staring at her, waiting for an answer. She shrugged her shoulders.

"She just asked where you were," she answered almost under her breath.

"Where was I?" I asked, racking my brain for a night that she could have possibly come in that I wasn't there. I worked every weekend that month.

"You had just left with Isabel," she nervously said. I felt a knot in the pit of my stomach. I could feel the blood rush out of my face. Of all the times she could have possibly come in here, she just had to choose the day I left with Isabel.

"Did you tell her that?" I asked awkwardly.

She looked to the ground, uneasy. "I'm sorry, was that a secret? I mean, the way the two of you left here that night, I didn't think you were trying to hide it." I looked from Kaitlyn to Max, neither one of them making eye contact with me. I suddenly felt like I needed to explain myself to Amber.

"Shit, I have to go. Can you guys finish closing up?" I asked, making my way around the bar, and heading towards the door.

"Are you going to try to get her back?" Kaitlyn asked.

"Do something romantic!" Max chimed in.

I stopped in my tracks and slowly turned around to face them. "What? Get her back?" I sluggishly asked.

Max raised his eyebrows at Kaitlyn, who bit her lip and looked down, her face turning red. "Don't tell me *that* was a secret. Everyone knew the two of you were together. You guys were so obvious. Everyone talked about it." I didn't respond. I just made my way over to Amber's club.

Chapter Twenty-Eight

The new club Amber worked at was only five blocks away, but I sprinted over there so fast I had to catch my breath before walking in. As I cautiously entered the bar, she was on the other side, her back to me, wiping down the counter. A few people lingered.

"Last call," she announced, looking up noticing I was sitting there.

We stared at each other for what seemed like hours as she unenthusiastically made her way towards me. Wearing ripped skinny jeans and a low-cut black shirt, she looked amazing – even with her hair pin-straight.

"I'll have a Jameson, neat, please," I ordered. She poured me the drink and returned to the other end of the bar as if I didn't exist. I drank the glass in one gulp and ordered another. She walked over to me, irritated.

"I said last call," she said, annoyed.

"Yeah, you said that because you had ten minutes left to serve, and I drank it in one," I said, lifting my sleeve and motioning to my watch. "Why don't you make me two this time, so we don't have to have this conversation again?"

She took out another rocks glass and poured me two drinks, then once again disappeared to the other side of the bar. She wouldn't even glance in my direction. I sat there, gradually sipping my drink and patiently waiting for the customers to depart. Once the last customer had left and we were alone, she still refused to meet my gaze.

"Hey, where's your bartender manners? A lonely guy, sitting by himself at the bar. Shouldn't you come over and see how he is?" I hollered across the bar. Unamused, she put the rag down on the counter and walked over to me.

"How are you?" She asked impatiently. I smiled.

"I'm good, thanks for asking – how are you?" She ignored my question and stared at me blankly; she was not happy to see me at all. I cleared my throat. "I, um – I heard you came by the bar a few weeks ago. I was wondering what you wanted."

"A drink," she said, no expression in her voice. I glanced past her to the liquor bottles displayed on the bar.

"Looks like you have plenty of Kettle One here," I observed.

"How's your Bella?" She asked, obviously still mad that I slept with Isabel. I let out an exaggerated sigh.

"Yeah, you were right about that one. Not a good idea; that didn't go well at all."

"Oh, really? I'm shocked," she said mockingly. "And how long did it take for you to figure that one out?"

"About twenty minutes," I said. "Forty, if you count

foreplay." She stood there staring at me, still silent. "Why'd you really come to the bar?" I pressed.

She looked down at my glasses, one full and one-half empty. "I need to close up, are you almost done?" She asked.

"Answer the question first," I said, lifting one of the glasses to my lips and taking the smallest sip possible.

"I was drunk and horny and knew you were an easy lay. And look at that – even easier than I had thought, I didn't make it in time. Trust me – it won't happen again," she replied.

"An easy lay?" I snickered. That stung. I may have slept around, but she was different. I never treated her that way when we were together. She knew exactly which buttons to press to get under my skin, and it worked. "Well, good thing I wasn't there because I wouldn't have slept with you. That ship sailed – far away."

I finished the drink and slid the empty glass over to her. Her eyes dug into me as if she were trying to pierce my skin with her glare. She hated me; she was so disgusted by the sight of me. I don't know if it was anger, or jealousy, or her lack of reaction, but I continued spewing out nonsense.

"You know, I'm not sorry I set you up with him. It doesn't bother me that he cheated on you. I don't regret not telling you. I don't care that you're not next to me anymore, and I *definitely* don't miss you."

She tried her best to smile as if it didn't bother her, but she couldn't. She looked right past me and said,

"Are you done?"

I took the other drink and swallowed it in one guzzle, slamming the glass on the bar. I took my roll of cash out and threw a fifty-dollar bill on the counter.

"Yea, I'm done," I said as I got up to leave. She took the money off the bar and went over to the register.

I had made it to the door, but just as I was about to leave – I heard my mother's voice: *Is she worth fighting for?* Then Andrew's chimed in, *I don't know what you did, James, but you better fix it.* And then Christopher's: *What do you have to lose?* Once again, the kid was right. I had even less to lose now. She was already gone.

I turned around to face her, her back still to me as she cleared out the register. "What if I was?" I asked.

"What if you were what?" She asked, still concentrating on the money.

"What if I was sorry that I set you up with him?" I asked, walking back towards the bar. "What if it does bother me that he cheated on you, and I do regret not telling you. What if it kills me that you're not next to me anymore?" I was now directly behind her, leaning on a stool. Silent, she refused to look up. "What if I miss you so much, I can't think about anything else? What would you say if I said all of that?"

There was a pause. "I'll let you know if you ever say it," she finally answered.

"Amber, please, look at me," I begged. She finally turned around to face me. "Come here," I pleaded, motioning to the stool in front of me. "I just need to tell you some stuff, and I can't do it with a bar between us. Just a few minutes, please. Just let me get this off my chest, and then I'll leave."

She put the money down and came around the bar. She stood by the stool next to the one I was leaning on. I sat down on it and pulled her closer to me, nestled between my legs, my arms around her waist. My eyes now locked in hers, I said, "I am so, so, so sorry."

She looked up at me, still no expression on her face. "What are you sorry for?" she asked.

"Everything," I said. "Every fucking thing from the minute I told you I'd be okay with you going out with him to knowing he cheated on you and not saying anything. To kissing you...."

"In Miami?" she asked.

"No, I'm not sorry about kissing you in Miami," I said as I pulled her into me and pressed my lips on hers. I kissed her as passionately as I could, praying she could feel in my kiss how much I loved her and realize how sincere I was being. When I finished, I slowly pulled my lips off hers. "No, you know what, I take that back. I'm not sorry about kissing you now either. But those other things I said, I really am sorry. You know, a few weeks ago, I watched all my videos, every single one of them."

"How long did that take you to get through?" She sarcastically asked.

"A while, but that's not the point," I admitted. "The point is you were right. That wasn't me. I don't know who that guy was, but it's not even someone I want to be. And the one video I did want to watch wasn't there. So, I deleted it. All of it, the whole iPad. A hard reset, they're all gone." She looked like she was searching for something to say. When she didn't say anything, I continued.

"Then one night when I was walking home from the bar, I saw that star. The planet, the one you told me about in the hot tub that night. I was thinking of the story you told me about with Venus and Mars and how they never ended up together, and I needed to know, did he even try?

That would be even sadder if he did try, and they still didn't end up together." I rested my forehead against hers. "You also told me that night that I was going to find someone who satisfied me so much, I didn't have the desire to be with anyone else, and I did. It's you. I don't want to be with anyone but you. I'm truly sorry about the entire clusterfuck of events I put you through. Maybe I wasn't ready to admit any of this, even to myself. I want you to be the person I go to sleep with every night and the one I wake up to every morning. Fuck, I even want to dance with you in the middle of the street and embarrass the shit out of our kids." She half smiled with that. "Amber, I love you."

She pulled away from me a little and shifted her gaze to the floor. I lifted her chin up with my hand. "Amber, please look at me. I have never been so serious or so real with anyone. Please, just look at me when I say this. I love you," I said again.

She let out a deep breath. "And what? You think you're going to come in here and tell me you deleted your porn like it's some sort of grand fucking gesture, and I am just supposed to fall in love with you again?"

"Again?" I asked with a glimmer of hope.

"Is that it? Are you done now?" She asked. I released my grip and let my arms fall into my lap. I thought for a minute.

Counting on my fingers, I listed, "I told you about the iPad, the Venus thing, confessed my love to you, yeah – I'm done now."

"I have to go count money," she said, ducking back behind the bar. I stood up from the barstool and ran my fingers through my hair. At least I couldn't say I didn't try.

I turned around to leave defeated when I stopped myself. I couldn't physically bring myself to walk out, not yet. I spun back to her, and in one final desperate attempt, I asked, "Can I walk you home?"

"I have to close up," she answered.

"I'll wait," I said, now sitting back on the stool.

"I can't serve you alcohol," she stated.

"I'm very familiar with the New York City liquor laws," I answered.

"Fine," she finally agreed.

It took her about forty-five minutes to close up; no doubt she was going extra slow just to torture me. As I watched her lock up and pull down the gate, I realized there was no bouncer.

"You don't have a bouncer?" I asked, surprised.

"Not on Thursdays," she simply said.

"That's not cool. What if I liked you so much that I wanted to stalk you? All I had to do is come here on a Thursday when there is no bouncer and follow you home."

"Concerned or jealous?" She asked. I remembered back to when she asked me that when I was questioning if she was really sick. Back then, I had answered "curious." No more games.

"Both," I admitted. She smiled as we walked towards her house.

"Were you busy tonight?" I asked.

"For a Thursday, yes."

"Did you do well in tips?"

"For a Thursday, yes," she said again.

"More than you make with me?" I asked.

"Yes." There was a pause.

"So, you want to come back to work with me?" I asked.

253

STEVIE D. PARKER

"Sure." It felt like the first time in a month I smiled.

"So. I'll see you tomorrow?" I asked as we got to her door.

"I have to give notice," she answered.

"Right. Okay, Saturday?"

"Two weeks," she specified.

"Two weeks?" I exclaimed. "This isn't corporate America; you didn't give me two weeks' notice!" She shot me a look. "Two weeks sounds fair," I said. We stood there awkwardly, staring at each other for a while. I didn't want to leave her. "Can I call you tomorrow?" I asked.

She laughed. "You're not going to call me tomorrow," she said assertively.

"Can I text you tomorrow?" I elaborated.

"You're not going to text me tomorrow either." She said it with such confidence; it was insulting yet incredibly sexy at the same time.

"Oh, I'm not?" I asked.

She shook her head. "No, you're not."

"How can you be so sure?" She came closer to me and stood on her tippy toes, and kissed me.

"Because you're going to wake up with me tomorrow," she said, pulling me into her apartment. I kissed her passionately as I pushed her towards the bedroom. I took my lips off her for just a minute to mumble:

"That's a good answer."

"You need to get over me," she said. I took my lips off her and looked at her, confused. "And I know the perfect way to do it," she continued. Dragging me towards the bed, she began kissing me again. "Rebound sex. Works every time."

She laid down as I got on top of her. I stopped kissing

her for a second.

"Yeah, about that, it turns out rebound sex doesn't work," I answered.

"It doesn't?" She asked, surprised.

I shook my head. "No, the last time I did that, I ended up right back where I was," I said, pointing my finger around her bedroom. "You know what I heard is good, though? Makeup sex."

She giggled.

"I'm serious," I insisted. "I mean, I never had it before, but apparently, it's when you have a girlfriend, and you break up for like seven months or so. And when you get back together, you have this amazing, mind-blowing, euphoric sex that the entire time, all you're thinking is how did I live thirty-six years without this woman in my life. So, as I said, I never did it before, but I'd be willing to try it."

She gazed up at me, wrapping her arms around my shoulders. "I wasn't your girlfriend," she said.

"I think we both know you were," I said, my lips reattaching to hers. "By the way, did you know that everyone at the bar thought we were together?"

She pulled her lips off me and looked up, with a look of shock on her face. "Really? I thought we hid that so well!"

I shrugged. "So did I!"

She clutched my hair through her fingers, as my lips sunk into her neck, my tongue trailing up to her ear. For the first time in months, I finally felt at ease, and I knew I was exactly where I was supposed to be.

"You know, I've been thinking a lot about Evan," I continued, lifting myself up and looking in her eyes.

"Stop- I don't have Jameson," she warned, still smiling.

"No seriously... he knew the whole time, he said it that night at the bar. He always knew I was in love with you," I said, in revelation. She ran her hand from my neck down to my chest.

"I'm pretty sure he was talking about me. He knew I was in love with *you*," she answered, pulling me by my shirt down to her.

"Either way, him cheating on you was the best thing that ever happened to me," I admitted. She stood still staring off for a minute, her eyes looking past me, as her brain retained my statement. Finally, her gaze met mine again.

"It's the best thing that ever happened to me too," she answered.

Chapter Twenty-Nine

FIVE YEARS LATER

"And that is the story of how James and I came to be," Amber concluded, placing her hand on my thigh. I put my hand on hers and looked over at Rob, sitting on the couch across from us, staring back at us dumbfounded.

"Story?" He scoffed, using air quotations. "That was more like a damn novel! Okay, I get it – you got your happily ever after. Amber got her dream wedding and writing career, James you got your house and your kids. So what is the actual point of this story? How does any of this pertain to me?"

Amber let out a deep sigh and shook her head, exasperated. "Speaking of my writing career, I have a deadline to meet. I'll see you guys later," she said as she stood up and made her way down the hallway. I turned my whole body and watched her as she walked away. All these years later and I was still checking her out when she walked away.

"Wanna know a secret?" I asked Rob, not shifting my gaze from Amber.

"What's that?" He asked. When she was finally out of sight and up the stairs, I turned my body to face him.

"I still catch myself starting fights with her every now and then, just to have make-up sex," I admitted as he took a sip of his drink. He chuckled, and no sooner had my lips touched my glass, I heard the shrieking of my very agitated daughter coming through the baby monitor, beckoning for Daddy. I took a sip and placed the glass on the coffee table.

"I'll be right back. Now I have two women bossing me around all day long," I said as I made my way up the stairs to Ariana's bedroom. I slowly opened the door and watched as her fake frown turned into an excited smile at the sight of me. I approached her crib as she stood up while holding onto it, jumping in excitement. I pushed her red locks away from her blue eyes.

"What's wrong, princess?" I asked.

Ariana started bouncing around more excitedly, pointing her little finger at me. "Da-Da Up!" She cried.

"No, no, not up. It's bedtime; go to sleep."

"Up!" She demanded, louder. She was so cute I couldn't resist her.

"Okay, but just for two minutes," I whispered as I picked her up and rocked her gently. Then, from the corner of my eye, I spotted my mini-me in the doorway. Rob liked to say Jake was his little person because of his brown eyes. Either way, I felt bad for all four-year-old girls around the world who had no idea that in fifteen years, there'd be a whole new generation of Nisan testosterone.

"You're up too?" I asked in a loud whisper. He wrapped his arms around his chest and gave me a mischievous, disappointed frown.

"It's not fair that you get to stay up with Uncle Rob and we can't!" He whined. I kissed Ariana on the head before lying her back down in her crib. I grabbed Jake by the hand and led him to his bedroom.

"Come on, back to bed. Uncle Rob will be here tomorrow morning, too," I assured him as I tucked him in.

"Promise?" He asked, smiling up at me.

"Yes, I promise. And I want you to promise me that when you wake up at the crack of dawn like you always do, you go straight to the guest room and jump on his stomach to wake him up," I said. He smiled widely at the thought of pouncing on him. "Now go to sleep. Goodnight," I reiterated, kissing him on his forehead. As I made my way back downstairs, I stopped at Amber's office and peered through the door.

"You really have a deadline, or are you torturing me by leaving me alone with Rob and his problems?" I asked.

"Both," she said through a smile.

"You're going to pay for that later," I warned, lightly biting my bottom lip.

"I sure hope so," she answered in a daring tone. I made my way back downstairs and once again sat on the couch across from Rob.

"Where was I?" I asked. He picked his drink back up and took a sip.

"These fish are relaxing to watch," he commented. "You were giving me an incredibly long, drawn-out tale of

Amber and James without getting to the point."

"Ah, right, the point," I said, picking up my drink and savoring a sip. "Rob, how long did your marriage to Brianna last? A year?"

"Fourteen months!" He argued defensively. He lay his whole body across the couch, resting his head in his hands.

"You know, I idolized you my whole life – wanted to be just like you. Now here you are. Forty-six years old, back in New York, lying on my couch like a lovesick puppy, asking your little brother for advice. Kind of ironic, no?"

He shot back up quickly, now sitting and glaring back at me. He hadn't shaved in a few days, and with his hair disheveled, he looked more like me than ever.

"And yet I still haven't heard it," he sneered.

"The point of the story is that if I didn't play so many games with Amber and just told her how I felt from the beginning, I would have saved both of us from seven months of torment and drama. You're in love, and it's new to you, and you're freaking out. I get it. I was there. But it's salvageable; you didn't do anything detrimental yet."

"So, what are you saying?" He asked.

"You know what I am saying," I stated.

"Do I?"

"You really want me to say it?" I asked.

"Yes."

"You really *need* to hear it?"

"Yes," he repeated angrily. I slid my hands down my thighs until they rested on my knees. Leaning towards him, eye to eye, I said slowly and with authority:

"Go get Mia back!"

Acknowledgements

Embarking on the journey of writing has been quite the ride. I am so appreciative of the wonderful writing community that has welcomed me with open arms. This would never have been possible without recognizing some very important people.

Thank you to my mother, who always had my back, no matter what I did in life.

Thank you to my nephew Christopher, who left this world too soon but will always be alive in my work and continues to inspire me every day.

And thank you to my circle of authors, who have become true friends. To Sara, Tanya, K.C., and Felicity, who have helped me with this book every step of the way.

I couldn't have done this without all of you!

About Atmosphere Press

Atmosphere Press is an independent, full-service publisher for excellent books in all genres and for all audiences. Learn more about what we do at atmospherepress.com.

We encourage you to check out some of Atmosphere's latest releases, which are available at Amazon.com and via order from your local bookstore:

Twisted Silver Spoons, a novel by Karen M. Wicks

Queen of Crows, a novel by S.L. Wilton

The Summer Festival is Murder, a novel by Jill M. Lyon

The Past We Step Into, stories by Richard Scharine

Swimming with the Angels, a novel by Colin Kersey

Island of Dead Gods, a novel by Verena Mahlow

Cloakers, a novel by Alexandra Lapointe

Twins Daze, a novel by Jerry Petersen

Embargo on Hope, a novel by Justin Doyle

Abaddon Illusion, a novel by Lindsey Bakken

Blackland: A Utopian Novel, by Richard A. Jones

The Jesus Nut, a novel by John Prather

The Embers of Tradition, a novel by Chukwudum Okeke

Saints and Martyrs: A Novel, by Aaron Roe

About the Author

Born and raised in New York City as a "nineties teenager", Stevie D. Parker grew up studying journalism. When life took her in a different direction, she spent the past two decades as a Public Relations Executive. A position that involved traveling throughout the US and dealing with many different types of people. A self-proclaimed "realist" with an astute sense of people and situations. She is fun loving, open minded and spontaneous but believes that everything happens for a reason. Passionate about everything she does, Stevie now spends her time writing fictional stories based on real life experiences.

https://www.steviedparker.com

Printed in Great Britain
by Amazon